What in the World Is God Up To?

What in the World Is God Up To?

God's Ultimate Plan for Humanity

MICHAEL M. CHRISTENSEN

WIPF & STOCK · Eugene, Oregon

WHAT IN THE WORLD IS GOD UP TO?
God's Ultimate Plan for Humanity

Copyright © 2022 Michael M. Christensen. All rights reserved. Except for brief quotations in critical publications or reviews, no part of this book may be reproduced in any manner without prior written permission from the publisher. Write: Permissions, Wipf and Stock Publishers, 199 W. 8th Ave., Suite 3, Eugene, OR 97401.

Wipf & Stock
An Imprint of Wipf and Stock Publishers
199 W. 8th Ave., Suite 3
Eugene, OR 97401

www.wipfandstock.com

PAPERBACK ISBN: 978-1-6667-3772-1
HARDCOVER ISBN: 978-1-6667-9748-0
EBOOK ISBN: 978-1-6667-9749-7

05/20/22

All Scripture quotations, unless otherwise indicated, are taken from the Holy Bible, New International Version®, NIV®. Copyright ©1973, 1978, 1984, 2011 by Biblica, Inc.™ Used by permission of Zondervan. All rights reserved worldwide. www.zondervan.com. The "NIV" and "New International Version" are trademarks registered in the United States Patent and Trademark Office by Biblica, Inc.™

Contents

Introduction		1
1	The Creation	16
2	The Turning Away	35
3	Reconciliation	55
4	Restoration and Glory Forever	97
5	Conclusion	108
Appendix A: A Brief Apology		113
Bibliography		117

Introduction

"WHAT IN THE WORLD is (the biblical) God up to?" If you've ever asked that question, you're not alone. It rings in the ears of many in our world, even among the followers of the biblical God. Why would anyone ask that question? Well, many areas of our world seem to be in disarray, and we wonder if it will one day implode—or explode!—and wonder if God is paying attention. Internationally, those in power are just as likely inept, arrogant, greedy, callous, or power-hungry. They live opulent lives while their citizens struggle to have enough to eat, have adequate shelter, or have access to basic medical care. Nuclear bombs are in the hands of the untrustworthy, many governments are thoroughly corrupt, and countries wage war with each other and kill indiscriminately—innocents, women, and children. Courageous citizens are shot dead in the street for protesting repressive leaders. Some cultures habitually mutilate the sexual organs of young girls or force young teenagers to marry for economic gain. Socially and relationally, illegal drugs incapacitate many, families are dysfunctional, adults overspend themselves into debt, kids and adults are mind-numbed by the many forms of electronic media, and marriage ends in divorce half the time. In developing countries, just feeding your family, having a roof over your head, staying away from disease, and avoiding murder by a radical faction is a lifelong challenge.

This does not mean there is not a lot of good happening. Countries send food, water, and medicine to other nations struck by floods, tsunamis, or earthquakes—no charge! International societies provide disaster relief, free medical care, and food and shelter to those in need. International travel has spawned greater appreciation of other cultures and fostered international cooperation and educational opportunities. Many countries run under the principle of law, and criminals are sought and punished. Religious and government agencies help the sexually or relationally abused, provide food for the poor, help the unemployed get jobs, provide inexpensive or free medical care, establish hospitals, care for the mentally challenged, offer counseling, and tend to the needs of the spirit. People still act like neighbors, looking after those who live next door, lend money to those who have had a tough break, treat the opposite sex with respect, and are polite. Adult children still care for parents who are invalid, and families still adopt handicapped infants or foreign orphans. Volunteers work for a multitude of religious or civic groups to aid those in their communities. People do work on their marriages. Addicts overcome bad spending or drug habits. Children do more than media—for many they go to school, study, do sports, join clubs, find a career, get married, end up independent, and contribute good things to this world.

The question is: Where is God in all of this mixture of apparent good and evil?[1] Does he supervise or motivate any of it? Even Christians[2] sometimes ask him, "What's the big plan here?" "Why do you allow evil to prevail in so many areas of life?" "Isn't it time to spank some people?" "Is pie-in-the-sky heaven our only hope of something reliably good?" Many also have questions about their spiritual lives and the behavior of Christian individuals and groups: "Why are effective servants cut down by cancer in the prime of life?" "Why do my fervent prayers seem to get no clear answers?" "Even with your Spirit inside, why is it so hard to overcome some sins?"[3] "How can you tolerate Christian leaders who cover up the molestation of innocent children in their care?" "Why do gifted servants wait and

---

1. "Good" in the biblical sense is some human attitude or act that intentionally agrees with and follows what God commands, wishes, or is the result of following one's conscience. It is obeying the two biblical Great Commandments to love God supremely and one's neighbor as oneself. Evil is a chosen attitude or act that disobeys such knowledge.

2. The name Christian is from the Greek *Christos*, which translates the Hebrew word *Messiah*, which means "anointed one." Anointing refers to the ancient manner of coronating kings, so Christians are followers of the anointed King and Messiah, Jesus of Nazareth. More specifically, Christians are persons who have recognized they have not lived their lives to please the God of the Bible and have humbly acknowledged they are estranged from him. They have turned from their selfishness and trusted that God will reconcile them to himself by accepting his offer of forgiveness and transformation through the death and resurrection of Jesus Christ. They are commanded to love God and not themselves supremely. They now have God himself, through the Holy Spirit, living inside them. Earnest Christians continue to live and deepen this reconciliation throughout their life. Christians differ in how deeply they love God, follow his commands, and represent him to the world. Some are shining lights, while others are a dim flicker. Only God knows the true state of each person's heart.

3. "Sin," like "evil," is a biblical word referring to humans knowingly disobeying what they know of God's commands and wishes or disobeying their conscience. James, the brother of Jesus, agrees, saying, "If anyone, then, knows the good they ought to do and doesn't do it, it is sin for them" (Jas 4:17).

wait while the church neglects them?" "Why do you wait while Christian leaders live double lives, and when exposed, hurt the gospel[4] message you want proclaimed?" "Why do you entrust the gospel message and the eternal fates of souls to sometimes incompetent witnesses (us!)?" "When will you judge Christians for living lukewarm lives, ones no different than the secular world they live in?" It seems God would have a more reasonable sense of moral and civil order. Does he love this world and his servants in it like he says he does? If so, then why doesn't he do something? We would. We would make it better. Or would we?[5]

Though as a thoughtful and studious Christian I have tried very hard, I do not have definitive answers to some of these questions. Sometimes I look to the heavens in frustration or anger. In my calmer moments, however, I can see rays of light that show me a path. I sense that the "big picture" that I live my life by is sometimes not God's "big picture." He values things that I count for little and I enlarge things that will soon pass away or are of secondary importance. So, what is God's big picture—and is anyone asking the question besides me?

WHO WOULD BENEFIT FROM THIS BOOK?

I have written this book for a number of audiences. First, to ones who have no commitment to the God of the Bible and from what they've heard and observed of his ways and the conduct of his followers, they really don't want to follow him. They need good answers—as far as we can give them. Second, to young Christians who have begun to face these questions in their own hearts or have challenges put to them by others. These questions may shake their faith. Third, to Christians in general who are trying to figure out the God they serve, want to love him more, and want others to love him too. Hopefully this book will be a good foundation.

No matter which category you fit in we need to clarify a few assumptions before we go further. First, I assume the Bible reveals the true state of affairs regarding the existence of the universe and us in it. It accurately portrays who God is, the human condition, and solutions to the problems of life faced by those in its pages, all those who live today, and all those who

---

4. Gospel in the biblical sense is the good news of Jesus Christ's birth, life, teachings, death, and resurrection in order to reconcile humanity to God. It proclaims he is the Savior of the world.

5. I think of the movie *Bruce Almighty*, where God (Morgan Freeman) gives a disgruntled Bruce (Jim Carrey) the chance to answer everyone in the world's prayers. Bruce doesn't do so well. With our limited view, we might not do so well either!

will ever live.⁶ Second, I do not assume my readers have a lot of biblical knowledge. However, you might have to do some digging and some looking up, but any treasure of real value requires that. God responds to those who seek.

OUR PATH

Whatever we know about God and his plans depends on what he reveals. This "revealing" has been general—our observations of the universe around us and the testimony of our own senses and conscience. God's revelation is also more specific—his acts through Abraham, Moses, and the nation of Israel; the coming to earth of Jesus Christ; and the books of the Bible—these are our most complete and objective resources for understanding God and his plans. A good starting point for understanding God's plans is to look at God himself—how does he describe himself? What are a few of his natural characteristics? What is his moral character like? These answers determine everything he does. If we don't accurately see who God is, then we will not understand his actions. I once heard a speaker say that "Satan is surely active in the obvious vices but his most potent weapon is in theology. His main goal is to deceive, to throw up a fog between God and humankind, and promote a false view of God so that the God we perceive we don't want anything to do with."⁷ I think this is largely true, and we will discuss these questions in this introduction. Next, to understand God's actions, Bible teachers have helpfully categorized what he has done throughout history and will do in the future. This "big story" is creation, turning away (the fall⁸), reconciliation, and restoration (heaven), and each will be covered in one chapter. These elements provide great insight into what God is up to.

---

6. I have included an Appendix A—"A Brief Apology"—to give a short defense of why we should even consider the God of the Bible as one we should ask the question of our book to. For how Christianity compares to other religions, see Corduan, *Neighboring Faiths*; and Samples, *A World of Difference*. For questions about the Bible's reliability, see Williams, "Are the Biblical Documents Reliable?"; McDowell, "Is the Bible Reliable"; Kitchen, *On the Reliability*; and Blomberg, *Historical Reliability*.

7. Harry Conn. Notes from a lecture.

8. The "fall" is the common word used to describe Adam and Eve's first sin and the effects of that on their posterity. It would be better characterized as a "turning away," and I will refer to it that way in the rest of the book. A fall suggests to modern ears somebody stumbling by accident; something we can't help. This is not a correct concept. Adam and Eve disobeyed God's explicit command, and everyone who follows in their footsteps disobeys conscience or whatever knowledge they have about what God would have them do. Everyone sins by choice.

First, creation is God's creating the physical universe and us in it out of nothing. Our earth was made fit for life, and it contained a paradise with flourishing plants and animals. We humans were specially made in God's image and were given the job to oversee all he had made. Harmony reigned over it all.

Second, the turning away is our first human couple, Adam and Eve, disobeying God's reasonable command, being expelled from their paradise (the Garden of Eden), and living the rest of their lives in a harsher world, with troubles and obstacles. Not only they, but *we* live in the same world where temptations to evil are common. We sense something supernatural about ourselves and our world, but it is definitely not paradise. However, if we look, we can see hints of God's finger.

Third, there is God condescending to us to save us from ourselves. We can not rescue ourselves from the moral mess we have made. He must do it, and we must respond by changing our mind about our rebellion and throwing ourselves on God's mercy. God's acts revolve around covenants with humanity to reconcile us to himself. This reconciliation is described by a kaleidoscope of words like "redeem," "renew," "justify," "heal," "save," "eternal life," "victory," "adopt," "restore," "reconcile," and "forgiveness." This metamorphosis is to continue and deepen throughout the Christian life, is fostered by our relationships with other believers, and is to be shared with the world so that many more will share in that life.

Fourth, there is the final restoration of both the physical world and those who are God's followers. Some Bible writers call this "glorification." This means this world is not the end of existence. God has planned an unimaginable future for those who have served him on this earth. Until that time all God's followers who die reside in a temporary but wonderful place called "heaven." It is a spiritual existence, but it is not the final home. Though our bodies die and decay now, the Christian will someday be resurrected after the final judgment of humankind and be united with what the apostle[9] Paul calls a "spiritual body" that will never die or weaken (1 Cor 15:35–56[10]). We will live in what the final book of the Bible, the Book of Revelation, describes as the "new heavens and earth" (Rev 21). We will be in

---

9. An apostle in the biblical sense is someone who was an eyewitness and follower of Jesus during his earthly ministry. Therefore, the twelve disciples who followed Jesus are called "apostles," as is Paul, to whom God revealed himself personally on the road to Damascus and whom God called to be a witness for him to Jews and especially gentiles (non-Jews).

10. There will be numerous references to Bible passages in this book, all coming from the New International Version (NIV) of the Bible. The standard notation for Bible verses is book, chapter, and verse. For example, the verses tied to this footnote are from the book of 1 Corinthians (1 Cor is a standard abbreviation), chapter 15, verses 35–56.

the company of all those who have loved God in this world. All those who have not chosen to love God supremely will also be together, but away from him. Jesus and other Bible writers call this existence "hell," and it is a place of regret and pain, away from all that is good.

All of the preceding implies something very important—God is going somewhere. History and our current world are going somewhere. We are going somewhere whether we know it or not—there is a goal to life! So, let's begin our journey and see what God has revealed about what he's up to. As the British say when ready to begin a task, "Let's get stuck in."

WHO IS GOD?

To begin to understand God's big story we need to find out who God is and what he is like. What we know about God is limited by what he has chosen to reveal about himself and by our finite abilities to comprehend him. But there are clear things he has revealed. The Bible talks a lot about what God is like, what he does, and his general nature and character. For our purposes five descriptions help identity him, and they are spirit, triune, love, holy, and subtle.[11] The first two describe his being, and the second two describe his moral character. The last summarizes his general method of relating to us. These ideas are strongly implied or overtly used by God and his followers to describe him. Let's look at them one at a time.

Spirit

Spirit refers to God's essence; Jesus declares this in John 4:24—"God is spirit." So, God does not have a physical body as we do. However, he has made himself known physically through various miraculous events or objects, his chosen servants, and most thoroughly through his son, Jesus Christ. The apostle John writes, "No one has ever seen God, but the one and only Son, who is himself God and is in closest relationship with the Father, has made him known" (John 1:18). The Bible further describes us humans as being in the image and likeness of God (Gen 1:26–27) and as being a spirit (Eccl 12:7). We can connect with him because in a finite way we are like him. We are spirit, and we are also physical, having a bodily form. Further, he

---

11. Many more adjectives could be used to describe the biblical God, and if you doubt that, just look in a theology book! God's attributes are certainly more than described here, but for the purpose of brevity and giving a basic foundation for what God is like and what he has done, these five are sufficient.

is personal and is always described with personal pronouns—God is not a "what" but a "who." Because we are in his image, we are also at root "persons."

Triune

Triune or Trinity further describes God's being—three in one. The first part of the Christian Bible, the Old Testament[12] (OT), mainly uses the transliterated Hebrew words *Elohim*, *Yahweh (Jehovah* is an alternate spelling), and *Adonai* to describe God, and they mean God or Lord. Second, the *Spirit of God* is spoken of early in the Bible (Gen 1:2) and is later referred to with the pronoun "he." The third member of this Trinity, the Son, Jesus Christ, was prophesied about as the coming Messiah or Anointed One who would save not only the Jews but all people from their sins. He is talked about in many parts of the OT, such as Deuteronomy 18, Jeremiah 32, Ezekiel 37, and Isaiah 9, 42, 52–53, and 61. Jesus inaugurated the new covenant, frequently called the New Testament (NT), and this covenant is explained in the latter part of the Bible. God covenants in a new way with humanity in which they are reconciled to him, and their sins are forgiven through the atoning sacrifice of Jesus Christ on the cross. The OT was temporary until the NT was begun. The NT makes it clear that Jesus is himself God (John 1:1–18). It frequently refers to the God of the OT as "Father" with Jesus as his Son, and the Holy Spirit as the Spirit previously referred to in Genesis 1:2.[13]

The true nature of this Trinity was discussed greatly throughout the Christian centuries, and several false views or heresies were rejected. It was concluded that this triune God has eternally existed in a wonderful relationship of *three persons with one essence*. Each in this Trinity seem to have different but complementary roles. The Father seems to function frequently as the head; the Son was a co-Creator and in history is humanity's redeemer and reconciler. Even now the Bible records that he intercedes in prayer for his followers (Rom 8:34; Heb 7:25) and is the head of his followers. The Holy Spirit frequently carries out the wishes of the Trinity, speaks to people's hearts about their true spiritual condition, joins with Jesus in

---

12. The Old Testament is the name Christians use to describe the first redemptive covenant between God and humankind; it began with Abraham and was fulfilled in God's relationship with the nation of Israel and their command to represent him to the rest of the world. Jews call all the books that describe the creation of the world and this covenant the Hebrew Bible.

13. In this book the singular pronoun "he" or the word "God" will be frequently used to describe the Trinity. This is a common convention and this will be my meaning unless the context implies otherwise. Quotes from the Bible or other authors likely have the same intent.

interceding in prayer for believers (Rom 8:26–7), and even inhabits the very being of Christians (Rom 8:11; 1 Cor 6:19). All this testifies that God is inherently relational and we are like him in this. God knows we do not do well alone—we need relationships (Gen 2:18), especially one with him. The apostle John states, "Now this is eternal life: that they know you, the only true God, and Jesus Christ, whom you have sent" (John 17:3). The apostle Paul says it another way—our sinful selves need to become new creations and reconciled with God (2 Cor 5:17–20). We also need good human relationships. For God's followers this is emphasized in places like Romans 12, where the apostle Paul compares the church to members of a human body. Each has different roles, and each is essential to the total functioning of the body. Together this body depends on each member to participate actively and to encourage and spur each other on to be better followers.

This triune nature of God is behind these actions to restore a broken relationship with him and, in fact, to restore the whole created world. The interaction of the three persons is described by an intimate Greek word, *perichoresis*,[14] which suggests a sort of circular motion or holy "dance" among them. Several authors relate this idea better than I can:

> Before the universe came to be, before the heavens were called forth with stars and moons, before the earth was carved in infinite beauty and human life was fashioned with style and grace and glory, before there was anything, there was the great dance of life shared by the Father, Son and Spirit. In staggering and lavish love, this God determined to open the circle and share the Trinitarian life with others. As an act of mind-boggling and astounding philanthropy, the Father, Son, and Spirit chose to create human beings and share the great dance with them.[15]

> Father, Son, and Spirit [are engaged in a] dance which is their life together, a dance without beginning and without end, a dance which is joy beyond all telling . . . The music of this eternal dance echoes in the vast reaches between the stars, pulses in worlds inside of atoms, travels on every breeze across the earth, and surges with the blood through our veins. From time to time, we hear the music of this eternal dance. During the silences when everything makes sense; during the celebrations when we taste a bit of heaven . . . when we are thankful for what we've been

---

14. *Perichoresis* is a transliterated Greek word which appears to be first used by Cyril of Alexandria, a fifth-century theologian, who was describing the interactions among the Trinity. It has been used ever since.

15. Kruger, *Great Dance*, 87.

given, proud of what we've done, hopeful about what the future holds. It is on these great and good occasions that we hear the music of the eternal dance, the rhythm of the Trinity. The Trinity is unending, joyous dance, yet the miracle is that the circle breaks open, and the Son and Spirit, still holding hands with the Father, extend their other hands to us, inviting us into the circle, drawing us into the dance, that we may become their partners, participants in their life.[16]

Hard to fathom—Father, Son, and Holy Spirit invite us into their very life! But one thing you might have noticed is that all these God-words are male—Father, Son, and Holy Spirit are described as "he." How can women relate? Is God male? Well, God exhibits traits most cultures would consider male *and* female. Also, both men and women are made in God's image. All this strongly suggests God is beyond male-ness. Then why is God always self-referred to as male? He doesn't really say, and most theories are just best guesses. It appears the role of father best expresses how he wants us to relate to him, and "son" best describes his relation to Jesus, the Christ. Regardless, we can continue to address God as Father, Jesus as Son, and the Holy Spirit as "he," realizing that the triune God has chosen these names for good reasons. We can trust their motives just like a child trusts a benevolent father.

Love

Moving on to God's character, we see he *is* love. He is not just love-*ing*, he *is* love (1 John 4:8, 16). All his actions spring from this motive—to love. But what does love really mean? Several transliterated OT words give us a better picture—the Hebrew words *ahab* and *hesed*. *Ahab* describes God's loyalty to the covenant he made with his chosen people, Israel; he is always faithful. He would never break his agreement or go back on his word to them. *Hesed* refers to love that never fails, is loyal, devoted, and kind. It helps those who are in need or helpless. One of the most revealing words to describe God's love is the Greek word *agape*, which is used in the NT. This love is other-serving, self-sacrificing, and is given even to those considered enemies. It can accomplish the great task of balancing justice and mercy. The apostle Paul in 1 Corinthians 13 summarizes other important traits—love serves others, is humble, is patient, is kind, is not easily angered, and is not boastful or rude. It encourages, protects, and provides for others' needs. It does not hold grudges (it forgives) and is always truthful. It hopes for the best and never gives up.

16. Author unknown. See DJimmyTst, "Perichoresis."

God showed this kind of love throughout his dealings with human beings. He was longsuffering in dealing with the sins of the people in Noah's day when most people's thoughts were continually evil. He spared Noah and his family and did not destroy humankind. He was likewise patient with the nation of Israel when their loyalty toward him was very thin. In another example, less than forty days after Moses went up to Mount Sinai to hear from God, the people down below were tired of waiting. They combined their gold and persuaded Moses' brother, Aaron, to fashion a golden calf for them to worship! He punished their idolatry but spared the nation because of his steadfast love for them. Later on we hear of the many times the nation of Israel was disobedient, worshipping the idols of neighboring countries. They exchanged the true God for false gods. Time after time God sent prophets to warn them, and when they didn't listen he sent judgment upon them so they would wake up, repent of their sin, and return to him. Most of the last books of the OT are these prophets' warnings to Israel. They repeatedly broke his heart, but he persisted in his love. God provided a great object lesson for his love is the story of the prophet Hosea, whom God used to show his people the extent of their unfaithfulness. He told Hosea to take a wife that both Hosea and God knew was an adulteress. Her name was Gomer, and Hosea was to have children with her. God instructed Hosea (whose name means "salvation") to give their two children specific names, which translated mean "not loved" and "not my people," signifying that God had ceased to love them and that he was rejecting them as his people. During their marriage Gomer was repeatedly unfaithful, just like Israel was to God. Yet God told Hosea to go to his wife, forgive her, and show love to her. He said, "Love her as the Lord loves the Israelites, though they turn to other gods" (Hos 3:1). Hosea even had to buy her back (redeem her, Hos 3:2) because while she was away from him she likely sold herself as a slave or became a mistress of another man. Like Gomer, eventually God judged the northern half of the kingdom (Israel) and told them they would be no more, but tempered with this judgment was his mercy in sparing the southern part, the nation of Judah. They had remained more faithful. Again, love shows itself in both justice and mercy. The *greatest* love shown to humanity was God's condescension to send his only son to earth as a final solution to the sin problem. This will be taken up more completely in chapter 3.

Holy

Holiness is another character word, and it flows from the one before—love. Holiness means God always does what is right according to his own being and character; he always does what is ultimately the most loving and what is true to himself. He does this flawlessly or perfectly. This implies God is separate from all that is not right. His holiness is so pure and complete that it is impossible for us to be totally exposed to his nature and character without being overcome. An example of this is the relationship between God and Moses in the OT. God warned Israel's leader, Moses, that the people should not look upon him while God's glory was resting on the top of Mount Sinai. They were to stay back (Exod 19). When Moses was ready to return to the people after forty days on the mountain, he asked God to show him his glory. God said he would let his goodness and glory pass before him but that Moses could not see his face, for no one could see his face and live (Exod 33). When Moses later received the two tablets with the Ten Commandments on them and was coming down the mountain, his face was radiant because he had been in God's presence. He had to put a veil over his face so others could tolerate being in his presence (Exod 34). The Trinity's presence was just as radiant when Jesus revealed himself to the apostle John in the book of Revelation. John relates his experience:

> *I turned around to see the voice that was speaking to me. And when I turned I saw seven golden lampstands, and among the lampstands was someone like a son of man, dressed in a robe reaching down to his feet and with a golden sash around his chest. The hair on his head was white like wool, as white as snow, and his eyes were like blazing fire. His feet were like bronze glowing in a furnace, and his voice was like the sound of rushing waters. In his right hand he held seven stars, and coming out of his mouth was a sharp, double-edged sword. His face was like the sun shining in all its brilliance.*
> *When I saw him, I fell at his feet as though dead. Then he placed his right hand on me and said: "Do not be afraid. I am the First and the Last. I am the Living One; I was dead, and now look, I am alive for ever and ever! And I hold the keys of death and Hades."*
> (Rev 1:12—18)

How, then, does a holy God like this deal with his created persons who rebel against his reasonable commands? His holiness and love push him to value both justice and mercy. To be totally just and punish commandbreakers every time they sinned would be fine if none or even a few sinned. But, given our freedom and the pervasiveness of temptation, we *all* have. Is total justice the best response? It seems not. God also wants to be merciful and show compassion on those who have broken his laws. But how can he do it without minimizing the importance and rightness of his very good laws and commands? As with love, we will discuss this conundrum for a holy God in chapter 3.

Subtle

The last trait we include is God's subtlety. This may seem counterintuitive considering the many miraculous events that are recorded in the Bible, but we must remember these descriptions cover large events in the creation, the history of the nation of Israel, the times surrounding Jesus and the first apostles, and the end of the world. For example, those manifestations seem frequent when reading the accounts of God giving Moses the Ten Commandments, delivering the people of Israel when he parted the Red Sea, Jesus' miraculous healings and deliverances, and his rising from the dead and ascending into heaven. The end of the world will involve God acting in more aggressive and intrusive ways to bring the evil that has plagued our world to an end. However, he is frequently not as obvious as these manifestations. In our current world there are no burning bushes, parting seas, saviors rising from the dead, or cataclysmic battles. Even when he is obvious, he seems to want to test us to see where our heart[17] really lies. Do we love him for who he is or not?

His subtlety likely has much to do with his intent with us. He has made us persons and has no wish to overwhelm us with his glory so that we have no choice but to revere him. C. S. Lewis has noted this. His book *The Screwtape Letters* contains fictional letters from the experienced demon Screwtape to his nephew Wormwood, a novice demon. Screwtape is giving him advice on how to keep people from living for God and instructs him on why God, the "Enemy," might deal with us in a subtle way:

> You must have often wondered why the Enemy does not make more use of His power and be sensibly present to human souls in any degree He chooses and at any moment... Merely to override a human will (as His felt presence in any but the faintest and most mitigated degree would certainly do) would be for Him useless. He cannot ravish. He can only woo. His ignoble idea is to eat the cake and have it; the creatures are to be one with Him, but yet themselves; merely to cancel them, or assimilate them, will not serve. He is prepared to do a little overriding at

---

17. What is the human heart? In our context it's not the four-chambered thing that pumps blood. It is the center or core of our self. It is the governor or determiner of what we value and cherish the most. When the word is used it frequently implies what we have given first place—what ultimately do we live for, and what motivates all we do? What is our first love? What do we worship above all else?

the beginning. He will set them off with communications of his presence which, though faint, seem great to them, with emotional sweetness, and easy conquest over temptation. But he never allows this state of affairs to last long. Sooner or later He withdraws, if not in fact, at least from their conscious experience, all those supports and incentives. He leaves the creature to stand up on its own leg—to carry out from the will alone duties which have lost all relish. It is during such trough periods, much more than during the peak periods, that it is growing into the sort of creature He wants it to be. Hence the prayers offered in the state of dryness are those which please Him best . . . He wants them to learn to walk and must therefore take away His hand; and if only the will to walk is really there He is pleased even with their stumbles. Do not be deceived, Wormwood. Our cause is never more in danger than when a human, no longer desiring, but still intending, to do our Enemy's will, looks round upon a universe from which every trace of Him seems to have vanished, and asks why he has been forsaken, and still obeys.[18]

Non-Christians have complained about God's subtlety. The well-known atheist philosopher Bertrand Russell was once asked after one of his lectures what he would say if he found himself standing before God on the judgment day and God asked him, "Why didn't you believe in me?" Russell replied, "I would say, 'Not enough evidence, God! Not enough evidence!'" Some wonder if Russell would have believed even with overwhelming miraculous evidence. Philip Yancey gives us some perspective when considering God's miraculous revelations to his own people, the nation of Israel:

> There were few, if any, atheists in those days. No Israelites wrote plays about waiting for a God who never arrived. They could see clear evidence of God outside the tent of meeting or in the thick storm clouds hovering around Mount Sinai. A skeptic need only hike over to the trembling mountain and reach out a hand to touch it, and his doubts would vanish—one second before he died.
>
> And yet what happened during those days almost defies belief. When Moses climbed the sacred mountain stormy with the signs of God's presence, those people who had lived through the ten plagues of Egypt, who had crossed the Red Sea on dry ground, who had drunk water from a rock, who were digesting the miracle of manna in their stomachs at that moment—those same people got bored or impatient or rebellious or jealous and

---

18. Lewis, *Screwtape Letters*, 41–42.

apparently forgot all about their God. By the time Moses descended from the mountain, they were dancing like heathens around a golden calf.

God did not play hide-and-seek with the Israelites; they had every proof of his existence you could ask for. But astonishingly—and I could hardly believe this result, even as I read it—God's directness seemed to produce the very *opposite* of the desired effect. The Israelites responded not with worship and love, but with fear and open rebellion. God's visible presence did nothing to improve lasting faith.[19]

Maybe, then, we should not feel left out when we read such words. Maybe the kind of trust God wants is not based on personally experienced supernatural-ness. Maybe God wants a response that springs from being vulnerable, courageous, and willing to persevere. Blaise Pascal, sixteenth-century mathematician, inventor, and Christian, agrees with C. S. Lewis that overwhelming human senses with divine majesty does not guarantee a loving response. In talking about God and his efforts to woo the hearts of humankind, especially through the sending of his son, Jesus Christ, he says:

> If he had wished to overcome the obstinacy of the most hardened, he could have done so by revealing himself to them so plainly that they could not doubt the truth of his essence, as he will appear on the last day with such thunder and lightning and such convulsions of nature that the dead will rise up and the blindest will see him. This is not the way he wished to appear when he came in mildness, because so many men had shown themselves unworthy of his clemency that he wished to deprive them of the good they did not desire. It was therefore not right that he should appear in a manner manifestly divine and absolutely capable of convincing all men, but neither was it right that his coming should be so hidden that he could not be recognized by those who sincerely sought him. He wished to make himself perfectly recognizable to them. Thus wishing to appear openly to those who seek him with all their heart and hidden from those who shun him with all their heart, he has qualified our knowledge of him by giving signs which can be seen by those who seek him and not by those who do not.
>
> There is enough light for those who desire only to see, and enough darkness for those of a contrary disposition.[20]

---

19. Yancey, *Disappointment*, 42–43.
20. Kreeft, *Christianity*, 254–55.

Peter Kreeft, in interpreting Pascal, states that if God did not conceal himself he would not reveal himself properly to us in our present state. Pascal's point is that God wants to move our will and not just enlighten our mind. God "further unveiled" would satisfy our mind and make it all but impossible to disbelieve. But that would hurt the working of our will, since one of the main goals is to humble our pride. An application of this is likely why God allows other religions to exist and spread—to make Christianity too obvious would make it too easy on the will; if we really seek we will see which God is the true one. Another application is the fact that good arguments seldom convince atheists, not because they are logically weak, but because they are *psychologically weak*. God lets us believe what we want. For example, if we don't want to see God in nature, we can neglect the design evidence and chalk it up to chance processes. If we want to exploit Jews (as in Nazi Germany), exploit slaves (African-American history), or get rid of "products of conception" (the pre-born), then we just view them as subhuman. We rationalize what we want to believe. We "self-conceal" God from our own hearts because *we don't want to believe*, and God lets us stay in that state until we are ready to change—until we are ready to be honest.[21]

Wow! That explanation gets at the heart of how God is trying to reach us. He woos; he doesn't coerce. Coerced love would be no love at all. He has thrown before us flecks of gold in the dust. He wants to be found, but he wants us to seek. It's like seeing a door cracked open at the end of a dark hallway—we see a light peeking out and want to see what is there. God beckons and wants us to open the door. Jesus said the following, just after he cautioned his disciples not to throw spiritual pearls before uncaring listeners (swine), "Ask, and it will be given to you; seek and you will find; knock and the door will be opened to you. For everyone who asks receives; he who seeks finds; and to him who knocks, the door will be opened" (Matt 7:7–8). That's the big picture of probably why God does not give us the undeniable "presence" we might wish for from him and why he makes us work to find him.

These traits are now the foundation as we look toward what God has done, the condition we and our world are in, and what direction he is leading this world. Our journey will take us through creation, turning away, reconciliation, and restoration. We begin where all stories start—the beginning!—in our case the creation of everything.

---

21. Kreeft, *Christianity*, 245–53.

1

The Creation

CREATION IMPLIES THE BEGINNING of something new that has not existed before. In the biblical context the creation is the beginning of the universe, to include our world and all that is in it—living and non-living, and even the concept of time. The major description of this event is in the first chapters of the Bible's first book, Genesis, which itself means the beginning or origin of something. These chapters tell the story of the creation of our world, light, everything in the sky (heavens), and the living things that inhabit our world. The process covers six apparent solar days, with God resting on the seventh. Consequently, some Christians use the genealogies in Genesis, and, assuming no gaps, conclude that the universe was created approximately six thousand to ten thousand years ago. Some Christians and many secular scientists say that reliable dating methods for both rocks and living things indicate the universe is over 13.8 billion years old and our earth is close to 4.5 billion years old. Archaeological discoveries suggest pre-human forms appeared millions of years ago, and what we now call our current human form, *Homo sapiens*, appeared about 200,000 years ago. Christians vary widely in how they interpret this data. Some hold staunchly to six solar days for creation and a six-thousand-year-old earth. They are sometimes called "young-earth creationists." Other Christians believe the universe was created by God but not necessarily in six days. Creation occurred over time, and the order found in Genesis is exactly the order we see unfolding in creation. They are generally called "old-earth creationists" or "day-age creationists" and have no trouble believing the earth is 4.5 billion years old and that humans have been around for much longer than six thousand years. Others believe Genesis 1–2 is not meant to be literal and its account is merely a story to explain that God is behind creation. Adam and Eve are not literal persons, and humans evolved from pre-human or more ape-like predecessors. When humans became aware of a spiritual dimension and the existence of a God varies.

HUMANITY

Regardless of the specific interpretation, most Christians believe God was the creator of the universe, he created it out of nothing, and we are beings able to understand that he exists and that we are able to know him. We are not only able to know him, but he wants us to. We are able to know God because we are created "in his image" (Gen 1:27).[1] This "image" quality is not specifically defined, but it likely includes our spiritual dimension—we sense there is a God and we have the faculties to know him. We are more than our physical bodies—if we die physically we still continue to exist spiritually. The concept also likely includes our charge from God to "be fruitful and multiply" and to "rule over or subdue the earth." We were to benignly take care of this earth and its creatures. We were to manage it all for good.

This image is further expressed in the concept of a non-physical "soul" or "spirit." We are a unit of body and soul while alive, but the soul or spirit lives on once we die; this is never said of animals. It appears our consciousness will also continue, so although we had a beginning at conception we will live forever in a "spiritual body." The apostle Paul talks about us being sown a natural body but raised a spiritual one (1 Cor 15:42–44). This body will be apparently more substantial than mere spirit, but everlasting, unlike our physical bodies. One everlasting abode is with God, and one is away from him; one is full of life, the other of shame and contempt (Dan 12:2).

As hinted above, we have consciousness and are aware that we are persons. We perceive other people as fellow persons, friends, and neighbors (or even enemies!). We are aware that we are unique and separate beings from other beings and can think, reason, feel emotions, and remember.[2] We have self-determination, can make choices among alternatives, and, within certain limits, determine our life's path. We can choose which desires to satisfy and which to not. We can choose what things to value. We directly

---

1. See Brand and Yancey, *Fearfully and Wonderfully Made*, chapters 1–3, for more on what being made in the image of God means.

2. See Moreland, "Arguing God," an interview with J. P. Moreland on the non-physicalness of this concept.

sense this. God frequently asked people to choose their life's destiny among alternatives. For instance, God asked the people of Israel to choose who they would serve: "This day I call the heavens and the earth as witnesses against you that I have set before you life and death, blessings and curses. Now choose life, so that you and your children may live" (Deut 30:19).

Relationships

The ability to engage in voluntary, committed, and continual human relationships is especially highlighted by God. He offers us a unique human relationship called "marriage and the family." An internal motivator to nudge us toward this kind of relationship is the attractiveness of the opposite sex.[3] This attraction develops in our youth, and as we go through puberty a strong sexual attraction usually ensues—strong enough to challenge our most well-held commitments. It is a desire God gives, but it was to be fulfilled in wisdom. If a man and woman love each other in a self-sacrificial and humble way, God blesses such a union—a marriage. It involves mutual love, submission, respect, and fidelity (Eph 5:21–31). In it each commits to love the other for life. It is a reflection of God's own love for us and of Christ's relationship to his church (Eph 5:32). This relationship involves intimate sexuality, which physically seals the union that has been committed to spiritually and volitionally.

So, what should this intimate marriage that God designed look like and point to? Philip Yancey writes:

> Lyrics from the love songs broadcast on pop radio stations tap into romantic yearnings but promise more than any person can deliver. "You are my everything." "I can't live without you." Sexual desires and romantic longings are a kind of debased sacrament. If humanity serves as your religion, then sex becomes an act of worship. On the other hand, if God is the object of your religion, then romantic love becomes an unmistakable pointer, a rumor of transcendence as loud as any we hear on earth.[4]

---

3 Some experience a sexual desire for those of the same sex. There is debate as to whether this desire is inherent or acquired during our lifetime due to our experiences and relationships. Regardless the direction of our desire or how it developed, God is concerned about what we do with our desires. His design was for marriage to be between a man and a woman. Sexual relations outside that commitment, whether they be adultery, fornication, or homosexuality, are not his plan, and he introduces sanctions against such to discourage them (Lev 20:13; Rom 1:26–27; 1 Cor 6:9–10).

4. Yancey, *Rumors*, 88.

Regarding sex, he states:

> We are never more Godlike than in the act of sex. We make ourselves vulnerable. We risk. We give and receive in a simultaneous act. We feel a primordial delight, entering into *the other* in communion. Quite literally we make one flesh out of two different persons, experiencing for a brief time a unity like no other. Two independent beings open their inmost selves and experience not a loss but a gain. In some way—a "profound mystery" not even Paul dared explore—this most human act reveals something of the nature of reality, God's reality, in his relations with creation and perhaps within the Trinity itself.[5]

Sex, in fact,

> lures us into a relationship that offers to teach us what we need far more, sacrificial love. Every married person I know wonders at times whether if he or she has married the wrong person. For that reason we need something more than a relationship built on emotions of the moment. We need something big enough to envelop circumstances rather than be enveloped by them. The old wedding vow sets out the commitment required of marriage: "for better for worse, for richer or poorer, in sickness and in health, to love and to cherish, till death us do part, according to God's holy ordinance..."[6]

So, God gave us marriage to bless us, to give us an experience of his own character, and to be the foundation for any children that would come into the world. The Psalmist David declares that children are a blessing (Ps 127:3). How are they to be treated and raised? Parents are to provide for the physical and spiritual welfare of their children. They are to model behavior that their children could follow and are to teach them how to live by word and example. If children want to stray from good conduct, parents have the authority to discipline them for their own good. The goal is to train their spirit, not harm it. The apostle Paul reminded the Ephesians, "Fathers, do not exasperate your children; instead, bring them up in the training and instruction of the Lord" (Eph 6:4). Children are also given guidance, "Children, obey your parents in the Lord, for this is right. 'Honor your father and mother'—which is the first commandment with a promise—'so that it may go well with you and that you may enjoy long life on the earth'" (Eph 6:1–3). The book of Proverbs states, "Listen, my son, to your father's instruction

---

5. Yancey, *Rumors*, 92.
6. Yancey, *Rumors*, 93–94.

and do not forsake your mother's teaching. They are a garland to grace your head and a chain to adorn your neck" (Prov 1:8–9).[7]

With or without children the family is the basic unit of human life. This union and the family were never meant to flourish without God at the center of it, and as a husband and wife mutually seek to serve each other the marriage and family blossoms (Eph 5).

Bible words in Greek for "love" suggest there are other very meaningful relationships that we can enjoy. Besides concepts for romantic love, *eros*, and familial love, *storge*, which we have already discussed, there is *philia*, a friendship love. Many of our most meaningful relationships are by friendship—comrades we had in wartime, neighbors we grew up with and still connect with, friends from school and college, friends who have walked with us through tough times or vice versa, or people we share common goals or interests with. God no doubt smiles on the loyal bonds we have made with people like these.

Emotions

This whole previous discussion has hinted at a feature of our humanness that we want to talk about directly. Humans have a rich emotional life and can experience great lows and highs. We not only experience them, but can communicate them through language, our gestures, actions, and the written word. God has emotions, and we read in the Bible about his emotional responses to what happens on earth. God is a spirit, so there is no need for a body to experience them, but our experience of them seems to include both spirit and body. These emotions can be both positive and negative. If we brainstorm we can remember many of them we have experienced personally. On the positive side there is love, joy, peacefulness, gratitude, hopefulness, contentment, pleasure, amusement and laughter, inspiration, and unselfish pride, to name a few. Common negative emotions are fear, anger, despair, disgust, loneliness, sadness, annoyance, shame, grief, selfish pride, guilt, envy, doubt, and jealousy. Since we possess choice, are finite, can make bad moral choices, and live in environments where sin exists, negative emotions exist. Positive or negative, they are a window as to what we are thinking about or to the state of our hearts and bodies. They are frequently responses to choices and attitudes either we or others have made or sometimes to circumstances. Relatedly, psychologists suggest if we want to feel a certain way, we should act first. If we want to feel loving, then we

---

7. This does not guarantee that every bit of parental advice is God-approved. These are general statements that parents are generally trustworthy guides for our lives.

should act more loving. The feeling frequently follows the action. In the same way, if we constantly dwell on how others have hurt us, it is no wonder why we would feel sad or sorry for ourselves. Emotions, whether positive or negative, were never meant to rule our lives. The choice to unselfishly love or to do good for its own sake is closer to the goal God has set for us.

A Body

Emotions do not exist in a vacuum; they are intricately connected to another wonderful way we exist—as a body. The human body is a physical testament to God's handiwork and is likely not part of what we would call God's image (as discussed above, God is spirit). Just one human cell (or any cell) has enough design elements to defy anyone to reproduce. All the cell functions, the organelles that carry them out, the ways it takes in nourishment, uses energy, gets rid of waste, and reproduces are beyond any human design. The complexity and intricate interactions among tissues, organs, and organ systems is beyond any chance explanation. We even have back-up systems! A look at modern medical textbooks will reveal what we humans have discovered so far about the human body and how it functions. No human being can understand it all—when we have physical problems we frequently have to see specialists, who study only one aspect of the human body's function. New discoveries are made so often it is hard to keep up and these testify to the great design and complexity of what we call our "selves." Our bodies are truly a marvel to behold.

In the end we are unique—we are "fearfully and wonderfully made," as the psalmist reminds us (Ps 139:14). Some have suggested that we are *merely* bodies; the things we can do—think, choose, feel emotions, move—are only manifestations of our physical brain, our nervous system, our muscles, and all our other organs. There is no "ghost in the machine." This is certainly quite different from the biblical view and contradicts our own consciousness.

A Moral Sense

The image also likely includes us having the ability to understand and make moral choices about the direction of our lives. God provides us guidance on the rightness and wrongness of something, and this is based ultimately on his own nature and character and about what he considers best for us and his creation. Right actions conform to God's loving wishes, and wrong ones do not. He communicates those wishes through his word (the Bible), prophets and leaders, and, for those who have access to neither, their consciences (Rom 2:14–15). From all these inputs we sense there are right and wrong attitudes and actions and we can choose which ones to obey. This choice was evident in the first humans—Adam and Eve—as God gave them a command to obey and they chose not to. Throughout the Bible God and his leaders asked people to make moral choices about their life's direction and expected them to choose him (Deut 30:14–2; Josh 24:15; Acts 2:14–41). If we choose to live in a relationship with God, we have the power to exude the virtues the Bible describes—love, joy, peace, patience, kindness, sexual purity, forgiveness, humbleness, self-control, mercy, justice, self-sacrifice, encouragement, thankfulness, wisdom, generosity, impartiality, sincerity, perseverance. We were created to live this way (Eph 2:10). We can also choose to exude vices, which are the opposite of these virtues. The difference between these two is not only outward but inward and involves our inner motives. Those who know God can display the virtues with a sincere heart. Non-Christians can also display the virtues outwardly, but their ultimate motive is not to glorify or love God with them; their goal is self-centered. Christians and non-Christians can also display vices when it suits them.

Other Image Qualities

We possess many other amazing soulish or spiritual traits that could reasonably be considered part of our nature or "image"[8]:

- A sense of the divine.
- The ability to sense and appreciate beauty.
- Curiosity.
- A search for our beginnings. Why else do we spend billions to adventure into space or to make repeated archaeological digs to investigate previous civilizations?
- Imagination—to create and appreciate what we create, be it a picture, sculpture, music, a story, a piece of technology, a new way to do something, almost anything!
- We appreciate humor.
- We laugh.
- Desire, sexual and for other virtuous and non-virtuous satisfactions.

---

8. Though some of these can be possessed by certain animals, we seem to possess the ones that overlap to an exceptional degree.

- The ability to self-sacrifice for another.
- A sense of responsibility and duty.
- A desire to be significant.
- The ability to forgive a betrayal.
- The ability to consciously end our own life.
- A desire to root for the underdog.
- A sense of justice.
- We hope.
- We engage in relationships that require continual (and optional) commitment.

Some of these overlap, and I could have listed more, but you get the idea. We are creatures with some amazing abilities that no other beings possess.

The Goal—To Know and to Love

We humans are marvelous creatures. We can do so much. God's goal is to have us use these amazing abilities to know him. It seems to be the whole point of our creation and its foundation is love. God loves the world he made and especially those in his image. He therefore desires the reciprocal response from us. The two Great Commandments of the Bible are declared in the OT and reaffirmed by Jesus, "You shall love the Lord your God with all your heart and with all your soul and with all your mind. This is the great and first commandment. And a second is like it: You shall love your neighbor as yourself. On these two commandments depend all the Law and the Prophets" (Matt 22:37–40). As the commands indicate, mutual love among humans is only next to loving him in importance. It is the way we were all designed to live. In fact, if we say we love God and hate others, we lie (1 John 4:19–21). The two always go together in God's eyes. That second commandment also assumes it is okay to love yourself. The apostle Paul assumed it was right to take care of ourselves and our own bodies (Eph 5:29). We are valuable because of who we are, and taking good care of ourselves is right and proper. You could say we are stewards of our own selves before God. If we are to treat our neighbors as ourselves, the assumption is we should treat both well! So, God's plan is to know and to love—him foremost, then others and ourselves.

How We're Wired

Because of the way we are made and the purpose God made us for we can see certain patterns of desires and longings that are built into the human heart. You could say we are "pre-loaded" to seek certain things out of life, and with some careful observation of yourself and others, you would probably come to the same conclusion as Daniel Strange, author of the book *Making Faith Magnetic*. That conclusion is that there are several "magnetic points" that every human being is drawn toward in trying to figure life out. These points are only adequately fulfilled in a relationship with God, but since God has given us moral freedom, we can choose to try to fulfill them with temporary and ultimately unsatisfying substitutes. The magnetic points are:

1. **Totality—a way to connect.** This is the issue of connecting with the world around us. We sense, and want to be a part of, something bigger than ourselves (a totality). We want to know what our place in the universe is. Yes, we know we are individuals, but we want to contribute to something bigger than ourselves, something significant. We wonder if there is something overshadowing that connects us all together for one big purpose. This "pull" is likely why we search for our roots/ancestry or why we join larger groups that share our interests and our priorities.

2. **Norms—a way to live.** A norm is a standard by which to live. We all live by certain norms, but we wonder if there are those that are for all people for all time (transcendent ones). Is there really a universal moral code of right and wrong? If so, what is that code, how can I find it, and can I actually live by it? Is it trustworthy? Can I depend on what many call an internal moral barometer—a conscience? If not, then does anything go? We all seek answers to these questions.

3. **Deliverance—a way out.** We sense we ourselves and our world are broken and we both need fixing or deliverance from what is breaking us (likely related to norms above). We yearn for an Eden, a paradise, a utopia, where everything is as it should be. If the problem is ignorance, then deliverance is knowledge/education. If it is illness—a cure. For loneliness—community. For poverty—needs met. For losing—winning. For fear—security. For confusion—clarity. For hatred or indifference—love. If it's death—life.

4. **Destiny—a way to control.** We often sense there should be some end goal or purpose of our being and that we should be able to control our fate. Control is good. Lack of it is bad and can lead to frustration or giving up. We certainly sense we humans have freedom and some

power to direct the course of our lives, but we're also aware some events happen *to us* regardless of our desires. There is a tension there. There are things that are beyond our control—our employer's demands, our spouse, our innate abilities and intelligence, our home culture and its norms, our opportunities. We may try to exert control through our use of every modern technology to achieve our goals, micromanaging every detail of a task, using lucky charms, using perceived higher powers such as gods or religion to achieve our ends. We may even humbly give control over to a higher power or person as we realize we are inadequate to control the important aspects of life. So, we try to achieve a destiny while balancing what we can control with what we can not.

5. **Higher power—a way beyond.** The other points end here as a source. We sense there is a higher power or person over the universe. There is a sense we should connect with this higher power—to transcend our current existence. World religions frequently, but not always, point to such a power or person. We give homage to this higher or ultimate reality, this something or someone of ultimate importance. Consciously or not we worship it—we give our heart to it. This attempt to transcend may express itself in reverence of our own selves (we see ourselves as the highest and most important beings in existence), an advanced civilization from another planet, angels or other supernatural beings, spirituality, the dead/ancestors, nature, the movements of the planets (horoscopes), religious experiences, religious sites, gods, or a God.

Similarly, N. T. Wright, in his book *Simply Christian*, states that humans universally have an innate pull or passion toward certain values or non-physical realities. He calls them "echoes of a voice." These four are the need and passion for justice, the thirst for a spiritual reality, a hunger for deep human and divine relationships, and a delight in and yearning for beauty. We find it difficult by merely living in this secular world to really understand or satisfy these "echoes," and Wright asserts it is only the Christian story that truly interprets and fulfills these passions.

Robert McGee, a Christian and professional counselor for decades, gleaned insights from his own practice as well as from many psychologists and Bible teachers to conclude that humankind has an innate need for significance, self-esteem, or self-worth. His book *The Search for Significance* delves deeply into the subject and shows this need is from God, and if we don't meet it through a relationship with him and fellow Christians, then we will seek second-rate substitutes. For example, we might seek significance through performance, seek approval from others, blame ourselves and others for our perceived failures, or resign ourselves to live in shame for past failures or bad habits we can't break.

Many religious leaders and even secular psychologists would affirm it is a human need to love and be loved and that these are basic requirements for any human to flourish. This seems to be a universally agreed-upon fact. However, these goals can be hard to reach on our own since we internally realize we never love anyone perfectly and sometimes it is difficult to find others who will love us for who we are. Who will love us unconditionally—who can we trust to love us without us being disappointed? And next, where can we find the power to love and respect others the way they ought to be? Can we even love those we don't like or who we consider our enemies?

We separate these "itches," "voices," and "needs" for clarity, but in reality they frequently overlap. One affects or relates to the other, and all hinge on their relation to a higher power. As human beings we try to make all these pieces fit together because there is no other choice—they are itches we can't help but scratch, echoes we can't get out of our head, or needs we can't help but try to meet. As we've seen, these authors suggest the only adequate answer to them all is a relationship with the biblical God. We may try to substitute lesser things in his place, but in the end only he satisfies because we were made to know him![9]

God Pays Attention—What Desires Are in Our Hearts?

With all these amazing abilities, the ways we are wired, relationships waiting to be deepened, and love commands from God, it seems reasonable that God is paying close attention to us who are in his image. He is very interested in how we live our lives. Some theologians reasonably maintain, then, that our time on earth can be described as a "divine probation," with probation defined as "the process or period of testing or observing the character or abilities of a person in a certain role."[10] However, he does not tempt anyone to sin (Jas 1:13) but wants all people to be holy like him. This earthly existence is a time to make us better. In this same letter to fellow Jesus-followers, James reminds his readers that they should "consider it pure joy, my brothers and sisters, whenever you face trials of many kinds, because you know that the testing of your faith produces perseverance. Let perseverance finish its work so that you may be mature and complete, not lacking anything" (Jas 1:2–3). God wants to test and perfect us. God repeatedly tested people. Initially he tested Adam and Eve. He could have put them in the Garden, let them do as

9. Strange, *Making Faith Magnetic*.
10. Oxford English Dictionary Online, "Probation."

they pleased, and given them no particular commands. However, he tested their hearts—he gave them positive commands and one "do not do this" command and allowed a tempter (the serpent) to have access to them. He did not shield them from the serpent's wiles. He allowed them to experience desires that they could overcome if they chose to, all the while watching how they would respond.

We surely do have desires. Human experience teaches us that we all have pulls toward both good and evil behavior. If you ask children how they make moral decisions, they may talk about a "good voice" and a "bad voice" in their heads. Whatever one decides to call it, we all sense this internal moral struggle with a sometimes intense pull from the evil side. The biblical authors do not put their finger on a definitive source, but they label desires toward evil as "fleshly." We also know there is the second influence of those around us who can tempt us toward evil (sometimes called "the world"), and, third, we have biblical examples of Satan enticing people to sin. Altogether these three combine to be potent influences and a significant test of what priority we will give God. Several Bible passages pinpoint God's active attention toward our behavior and the place of testing in our earthly life:

Moses speaking to the nation of Israel before they entered the Promised Land:

> Remember how the Lord your God led you all the way in the wilderness these forty years, to humble and test you in order to know what was in your heart, whether or not you would keep his commands. (Deut 8:2)

King David speaking to his son:

> And you, my son Solomon, acknowledge the God of your father, and serve him with wholehearted devotion and with a willing mind, for the Lord searches every heart and understands every desire and every thought. If you seek him, he will be found by you; but if you forsake him, he will reject you forever. (1 Chr 28:9)

David speaking again:

> The Lord looks down from heaven on all mankind to see if there are any who understand, any who seek God. (Ps 14:2)

God speaking:

> I the Lord search the heart and examine the mind, to reward each person according to their conduct, according to what their deeds deserve. (Jer 17:10)

Other examples follow the same pattern. Consider Abraham: "Sometime later God tested Abraham" (Gen 22:1) by asking him to sacrifice his only son Isaac as a burnt offering on Mount Moriah. Since Abraham knew this command was from God, he obeyed, but no doubt with the hesitancy we all would have at such a seemingly un-Godlike request. When Abraham had the knife raised the angel of the Lord stopped him, saying "Now I know that you fear God, because you have not withheld from me your son, your only son" (Gen 22:12). God wanted to see if Abraham was trustworthy enough to receive the blessing he wanted to give him—to multiply his descendants greatly and to bless the nations through him (Gen 22:16–18). In another example, God allowed Job to be tested. Satan asserted that Job served God because God had been good to Job—remove all of his blessings and Job would curse God to his face. So God gave Satan permission to afflict Job's family, possessions, and even his body to show Satan how Job would respond. God tested Hezekiah to see what was really in his heart (2 Chr 32:32). God tested the nation of Israel as a whole numerous times to see if they would obey his commands or not—during their wilderness wanderings (Exod 16:4; Deut 8:2), with false gods and prophets (Deut 13:3), and after Joshua had died (Judg 2:21; 3:4). He did this to help his people remove spiritual impurities (Ps 66:10; Jas 1:1–4). Jesus tested Philip's thoughts on Jesus's power by asking him how they were to feed five thousand men (John 6:5). Peter and James counseled their hearers that they should rejoice even though they experience grief and trials, which God uses not to harm or discourage but to encourage perseverance and to test, refine, and mature their faith. This fruit of faithful and mature children will result in praise and glory to God when Christ returns (1 Pet 1:6–7; 4:12–13; Jas 1:2–4).

This all shows that God not only wants to know what is in our hearts, he wants to bring about good things from testing those hearts. He wants us to rise to the occasion and respond with trust, love, dependence, and obedience. As mentioned before, we must recall that it is neither necessary nor desirable that sin should be the cause of testing. Paul squashed the thinking that sin should be used to bring about good (Rom 3:8). However, it seems that desires, which allow temptation to occur, are elements God has allowed in our being in order to test and perfect us.

Work and Rest

Another important aspect of being a human in God's image is what we do with the time we are on this earth. *What are we to do?* Does God care how we spend our time, and if so, what should we spend it on? This topic relates to the idea of work. From the very beginning God gave humans tasks to accomplish that contributed to the welfare of this world. Adam and Eve were tasked with tending the Garden of Eden (Gen 2:15). Two of their offspring, Cain and Abel, were shepherds and farmers, respectively. Work is inherently necessary, today as then, since our daily needs of food, clothing, and shelter continue. We either need to provide these items for ourselves directly (if we happen to be skilled at farming, sewing, and construction and have some way to provide the raw materials for all of that—a tall order!) or we need to have some skill or ability that allows us to trade the value of that skill for the necessities of life. Frequently money or some barter system is the intermediary. This is all quite obvious to most adults, although some think they can get by in life by not working or by trying to live off of the government or rich relatives. The biblical view wants us to be more independent. Hear what the apostle Paul tells the Thessalonian Christians in his letter to them: "Make it your ambition to lead a quiet life: You should mind your own business and work with your hands, just as we told you, so that your daily life may win the respect of outsiders and so that you will not be dependent on anybody" (1 Thess 4:11–12). In a subsequent letter he reiterates that it is not good to be idle. We should work so that we are not a burden on others and so that we provide a good example. He concluded, "For even when we were with you, we gave you this rule: 'The one who is unwilling to work shall not eat'" (2 Thess 3:10). Not only are we to work to provide for ourselves and our families, but to also have resources to help others in need (Eph 4:28).

So, what goal does God want us to shoot for as we choose and continue with our work? There appear to be certain values that work generates. Many lines of work provide some good or service that helps humanity to function in a modern world. They also provide opportunities for persons to develop valuable social relationships. We get practice cooperating with those above, below, or at our same hierarchy level. We learn how to work together to accomplish a common task. It further allows us to use our special talents or gifts where they can best shine. We all have things we are good at, and it makes sense to use these abilities as often as possible—and what requires our time and effort more than our daily work? A last idea is that work is important because it is valuable in and of itself. It is intrinsically a good thing to do. It is something God does, and this is likely an outflow of our very nature and being in his image. These conclusions are inferences as one looks at God's overall plan for humanity, which is that we should all live in harmony as we serve him and value our neighbor as we value ourselves. When done with that attitude work will have its truest meaning and fulfillment.

Ethics and Work

There has always been a discussion about the propriety or not of certain types of work. It is obvious that certain professions call one to engage in activities that go against the general ethical commands of the Bible. For instance, prostitution goes against the commands against fornication and adultery, so it is not a viable line of work for someone who wants to please God. If lying was part of a job's requirements, that would go against the command to not bear false witness (Exod 20:16; Prov 12:22). Selling things that are obviously harmful to humans, like illegal drugs, would be counter to God's command to love our neighbor. Dealing in the sale of something like alcohol, although legal, seems to have little redeeming value for the Christian—it can be neutral at best to causing great harm at the worst. There are other professions like gambling, or participating in gambling, which are highly questionable. The nature of the word is even against what we would consider work—you are using very poor odds in the hopes of getting a large payout. This is, at best, a desperate quest to make money where more legitimate ways are available. It is assumed that no matter what line of work a person chooses that it would be performed understanding that God is looking at our heart while we do it. His ultimate goal was that any work be done to honor him and to serve humankind. When done in this way it is a great blessing.

Rest

Finite beings that we are, we can not work continuously. Our bodies and spirits need rest to function well. Rest was built into the very nature of creation as the story unfolds in Genesis—God worked six days to create the universe and rested on the seventh. The word that is translated "rest" in English can also be translated as "to cease work." This is more likely the meaning here, as God is not a physical being who needs to rest because his muscles are tired or his blood sugar is low. However, we do fit in that category, and rest is a definite need, both daily, weekly, and on other occasions. We need to be refreshed regularly, and when we are not we do not function well. Rest is a built-in need for us; it allows us to truly re-create—to make ourselves new. It is also good for our souls. We need to rest our minds, to let our emotions settle, let our bodies recover (or maybe move more!), and to think of other things besides our daily routines. It gives us regular time to reflect on God, our relationship with him, and the direction our lives are going.

ANGELS AND DEMONS

As we read the Bible we discover there are other created beings, spiritual beings, who were created before we were and who communicate with God, serve him, and frequently act as messengers or intermediaries to carry out his wishes on earth. They also worship God before his throne in heaven. They're called angels. Hebrews 2:17 says we were made "a little lower than the angels," signifying their elevated nature and abilities. The Bible records a number of human encounters with angels in both testaments and of some we even learn their names—Gabriel and Michael, for instance. It appears that in the past Lucifer and other angels rebelled, losing their angelic role, were consigned to the earth, and received a new name—demons. Lucifer, a name that means "morning star," rebelled against God (Ezek 28; Isa 14:12–17) and was subsequently named Satan ("the adversary") or the devil. Now he and his demons work against God's kingdom, trying to undo the good Christians are attempting to do, lead people away from God, and falsely accuse humankind of evil. It is thought Satan was embodied in the Garden of Eden when the snake tempted Adam and Eve to eat from the tree and also came before God to accuse Job of unholy motives. He is mentioned more in the NT than the OT and has confrontations with Jesus on several occasions, always losing. He has the power to influence but not to cause someone to do evil. He actually possessed people in the Bible, and Jesus and his first disciples cast his demons out of them on several occasions (Luke 4:31–37). Even today, demons can take possession of persons who give them permission and who yield their wills repeatedly to them.[11] It takes the power of God and servants of God to release them. It appears Satan will continue his rebellion and subversive campaign against God and his servants until the very end of earthly history. He is the enemy described in the last book of the Bible, Revelation, and is defeated and thrown into the lake of fire (the final hell) forever. However, he and his demons are very active now and will be until then.

NON-HUMAN CREATION

Our discussion of humanity and angels certainly does not exhaust what God made. He created everything that exists. When we look at the sky, especially with modern technology, we see the vastness of the universe. Modern telescopes allow us to see many stars and nebula in our own Milky Way

---

11. See Blake, "When Exorcists"; and Arnold, *3 Crucial Questions*, for modern-day stories.

galaxy. Reaching out further, some telescopes have pierced the dark areas of space and found a myriad of galaxies there. Scientists currently estimate there are one hundred billion stars in our galaxy and over two trillion galaxies in the observable universe. We have no reference point for these huge numbers! And why do we think they are beautiful? After all, they're just burning masses of gas, right? What is it about looking at the sea of stars or the ribbon of the Milky Way on a dark night? Or the Northern Lights? Or the Crab Nebula? Why do we look in awe? It's because they are more than an accident.

When we draw closer to our own solar system and planet Earth, we see even more clearly the hand of a Designer. Our earth happens to be in just the right kind of galaxy, at the right position in that galaxy, orbiting the right kind of star at just the right distance, with just the right tilt, having just the right water-to-land-mass ratio, having just the right layers of atmosphere to protect us, with an effective magnetic field, with neighboring comet-sweeping planets, very far from a black hole, and one with a solitary moon. All these factors being just right make life possible, and conservative odds of that happening by chance are one in 1×10^{17}.[12] Chance is not a reasonable option.[13] It seems God is giving us a nudge that says, "Hey, I am behind all that you see." Sometimes we wonder if we are the only worlds God created with image-bearers. Consider the vastness of his universe. No one knows, but it would not be a surprise if he created other worlds like ours. He just hasn't let us in on it!

Living Things

Going down to the surface of our Earth, the intricateness escalates. God's story is written in the very existence of plants, animals, and the nature of their interactions.[14] Plant photosynthesis is a marvel of energy creation, and spore or seed reproduction uses wind, water, and even animals to send them to new growing areas and to ensure their continued existence. Animals (and humans) can eat plants and use their energy (How did that happen?). Animals themselves vary from insects to invertebrates to vertebrates; some are cold-blooded and some warm. Warm-blooded animals have sophisticated systems to keep them warm and insulated with effective blood-pumping

---

12. Clayton, *Source*, 21–28.

13. Resources on God and the physical universe include: Bussey, *Signposts*; and Dembski and Kushiner, *Signs of Intelligence*. A more basic book is Clayton, *The Source*.

14. Some suggested resources on this topic are: Rana, *The Cell's Design*; and Brand and Yancey, *Fearfully and Wonderfully Made*.

hearts and lungs that keep them all going. Each plant and animal seems to play a part in the whole scheme of the web of life. Each provides a unique expression of life, and frequently other creatures need these for their survival. Certain insects only pollinate certain flowers. Certain animals only eat a small variety of plants or other animals. Some animals eat only other animals, and the rarest are at the top of what we call the "food chain." The chain only flourishes if each link is present. The study of this whole system of how organisms relate to their environment and other creatures is called "ecology," the study of which testifies to the interconnectedness of our physical earth to each living thing. These relationships are far beyond a chance occurrence. It has all the earmarks of intricate design. It is another maybe-not-so-subtle revelation of God telling us he is behind it all.

We all can see that the natural world is filled with both great complexity and beauty. Most of us enjoy a majestic sunset, a mountainpeak view, or a quiet walk in a cool forest. This appreciation of nature is expressed often in music—just listen to the songs of John Denver. We just sense there is something good about nature and its creatures. When we want to recreate (which means to create anew, give new life, bring freshness to), we don't go to the concrete jungle—we immerse ourselves in nature. Why do we do this? Why does nature have a pull on us? It is supposed to. It is a testimony to its Creator. Job in the OT says this, "But ask the animals, and they will teach you, or the birds in the sky, and they will tell you; or speak to the earth, and it will teach you, or let the fish in the sea inform you. Which of all these does not know that the hand of the LORD has done this? In his hand is the life of every creature and the breath of all mankind" (Job 12:7–10). This is King David in Psalm 19:1–6:

> *The heavens declare the glory of God; the skies proclaim the work of his hands. Day after day they pour forth speech; night after night they reveal knowledge. They have no speech, they use no words; no sound is heard from them. Yet their voice goes out into all the earth, their words to the ends of the world. In the heavens God has pitched a tent for the sun. It is like a bridegroom coming out of his chamber, like a champion rejoicing to run his course. It rises at one end of the heavens and makes its circuit to the other; nothing is deprived of its warmth.*

We are part of something bigger. It is another witness that God exists, that he is behind all that we see, that he is loving and good and wants us to respond in kind.

SUMMARY

What can we say so far about our question—What in the world is God up to *by creating the universe*? He made things that were good and awe-inspiring and that came from his own desire to share his love. This is best seen in our own creation. This is the height of love, to give something of who you are. Genesis says Eve was created from the rib of Adam, and this parallels what God had already done by making both of them in his image—are we not also from the "rib" of God?

And so, at the end of God's creating all was right with the world. Our world was pristine, filled with goodness and brimming with hope. Would our world continue on the good path God set it on? As we saw a crack had begun to form. Satan and his fallen angels had gone their own way against God and were trying to entice his image-bearers to do the same. We skipped ahead a little in this chapter when discussing things like sin, evil, and vices in order to show some of the features of our design and the situation we all currently face. That story—the story of how our world lost its innocence—is next.

2

The Turning Away

THE IDYLLIC WORLD THAT God had created was now complete. Creatures made especially in his image were now in a wonderful Garden with all they needed to make life rich. Animals and plants filled the world and they were given purposeful tasks to accomplish. As mentioned earlier, however, God left Adam and Eve with a "do not do this" command regarding picking the fruit of certain trees, warning that disobedience would result in death.[1] He also allowed the serpent access to them. Further, we know part of God's strategy with humanity was to see what they would do with their freedom—would they continue to love and obey him or choose their own path? They had desires that could be managed for good or perverted. Satan, as the serpent, questioned the goodness of God's command and encouraged them to doubt God and his good will toward them, saying,

> "You will not surely die . . . for God knows that when you eat of it your eyes will be opened, and you will be like God, knowing good and evil." When the woman saw that the fruit of the tree was good for food and pleasing to the eye, and also desirable for wisdom, she took some and ate it. She also gave some to her husband, who was with her, and he ate it. Then the eyes of both of them were opened,

---

1. Death means the cessation of or separation from life. Adam and Eve's disobedience brought about immediate spiritual separation from God; their relationship was now broken. It is also possible that eventual physical death was a part of the consequence of that disobedience. Sometimes the Bible's writers use the word "death" to mean both. We will try to clarify as much as possible as to which aspect the usage refers.

and they realized they were naked; so they sewed fig leaves together and made coverings for themselves. (Gen 2:4–7)

Something very significant had just happened—the perfect world was no longer so. The most sacred relationship humankind had was now broken. Sin had entered. Yes, their eyes were opened, but it was not wisdom they gained, but surely it was a kind of "knowledge of evil" they had not intended. Now they knew what evil was. Yes, they had been lied to, but they walked into the deception willingly. And what frequently happens when one sin is committed is that others follow on its heels to cover it up. For what happens next? When confronted by God Adam blames Eve for giving him the fruit and Eve blames the serpent for tempting her! How typical of what still happens today—"It's not my fault!"

There was more fallout to come. Likely because God did not want them to now eat of the tree of life and live forever in this sinful state, and because they had now scorned his command and the benefits of his Garden, God banished the pair. They were sent, and this is the origin of the phrase "east of Eden." Now Adam would have to toil to raise crops, because now there would be weeds and thorny plants to contend with, and there would be no more water coming up from the ground to water the plants. Eve would have greatly increased pain in childbirth, and "your desire will be for your husband, and he will rule over you" (Gen 3:16b).[2] Still today we experience the repercussions of those first sins. Women still have great pain in childbirth, and every farmer and gardener must fight with weeds, insects, underground pests, and weather to bring about a worthwhile harvest from the seeds they sow. Even if we are not farmers, work is generally hard—physically, mentally, emotionally, or a combination thereof.

But the largest consequence was now that death became a reality for us. The apostle Paul said, "The last enemy to be destroyed is death" (1 Cor 15:26). It's an enemy because it is against all that God has for us. It separates us from him now if we are not one of his own. It will separate us from him eternally if we physically die without loving him. The creature, made in the Creator's image, separate from him forever; that is truly a most horrible thought. The only thing remotely comparable would be a parent who, after many attempts to get a wayward child to reconcile, is finally told to "stay out

---

2. Some Christians hold to a view that Adam and Eve's "original sin" produced internal negative consequences for all human descendants. This idea holds that now humans are not born innocent, but are born spiritually dead; they are born with a severed relationship with God. Further, their nature is tainted such that they can do nothing but sin. Goodness is not even possible in this natural state. For a critique of this view see Christensen, *God, Adam, and You*. The author's view is that spiritual death is the result of our own sin, not Adam's.

of my life." The separation is not only vertical, but horizontal. All our human and earthly relationships are stained by the separation that comes from sin.

This sin pattern continued in the next generation as Adam and Eve's sons, Cain and Abel, bring offerings to God to honor him. We do not know the details of exactly why Cain's offering was displeasing to God, but Cain became angry and took his brother into a field and slew him there. We can speculate about a motive, such as jealousy, revenge, hurt pride, or anger at God, but ultimately a personal desire trumped what pleased God most. Now murder and its guilt were a part of the human experience. Cain was then banished from the land he farmed and sent into exile and disgrace because of his sin.

The sin pattern has continued to the present. All persons described in the Bible sinned. We have all sinned according to God's evaluation: "Indeed, there is no one on earth who is righteous, no one who does what is right and never sins" (Eccl 7:20). "If we claim to be without sin, we deceive ourselves and the truth is not in us" (1 John 1:8).

DESIRE

As we hinted at before, behind all sin there is a desire—for something inappropriate in God's eyes. Adam and Eve ate because of the desire for the serpent's kind of wisdom, for food in their belly, and because the fruit was "pretty." Cain murdered out of anger and possibly jealousy or revenge. Motives can be almost endless, but they all center on self supremely. Early theologians called these desires "inordinate," which means unhealthy and obsessive. One could say people "worship" the object of their desire; they live to see it satisfied. Most desires can also be "ordinate" when they are fulfilled under the umbrella of God's commands and wishes. For instance, we can appreciate beauty and enjoy its presence in a person, a landscape, or a work of art. But we can be so enamored with our own beauty that we can't be happy unless we think we are the most beautiful. Or we can try to raise the most beautiful flowers, and to achieve that we break the rules in a flower contest, bribe a judge, or sabotage the other entrants. We may also have a desire to be a leader and influence a family, a company, or an organization for the good of all involved. That seems pretty ordinate. But let's say we really like the feeling of power that positions of leadership provide and we want to exert it all by ourselves with little input from others, since they are not as able as we are. We want to have all others, in a figurative sense, bow to our wishes. That is inordinate. Inordinate desires are summarized well by James, the brother of Jesus, in his letter, "But each one is tempted when, by his own evil desire, he is dragged away and enticed. Then, after desire has conceived, it gives birth to sin; and sin, when it is full-grown, gives birth to death" (Jas 1:14).

So, let's do an experiment. Take the last disagreement you had with someone, and think impartially about what caused it. Was it caused because both parties were so loving that they just had to fight? Or was it something else, something more personal, more me-centered, that was at the root? At the root of all sin is desire gone amok.

Desire Gone Amok—The Nature of Sin

There was a Christian evangelism tract popular in the 1970s and 1980s developed by Campus Crusade for Christ (now called Cru). It was titled "The Four Spiritual Laws" and was used to help evangelize people for Christ.[3] One of the laws was that we were sinful and separated from God and that was because "Self" was on the throne of our heart. There was a picture of a throne with a big *S* sitting on it. It was an accurate description of the nature of sin. We discussed the definition of sin earlier and said it was willful disobedience to what we knew God wanted or what our conscience revealed to us. The "why" of that disobedience is life centered around "me" supremely. This is desire gone amok, which can go in several directions. You can go the sensual route—pleasure reigning supreme. Think of food, sex, drugs, extreme sports—anything that stimulates the senses. Rebellion or unbelief is common. As the child says to a parent, "You're not the boss of me!" Authority is there to be challenged. "Nobody has a right to tell me what to do, and for sure nobody is going to shove religion down my throat!" Unbelief could show itself by requiring God to show himself with one-hundred-percent surety to our senses, something he's never promised. Then there's an old but accurate word—"idolatry," which is worshipping something else besides God. Some worship their bodies, youth, their spouses, money, possessions, status, being liked, their own rights, or spirituality where they always get what they ask for. These overlap, but they're all versions of self on the throne.

The big *S* can be seen in how leaders in governments or organizations rule their people. If your philosophy revolves around only a few having control (an oligarchy), in the selfish version those being ruled would be shorted in some way because they are not the most important thing—the leaders are. When citizens naturally challenge that authority leaders must be coercive to protect their interests. The following are things that usually happen: People can't leave without our permission (seldom or never granted). We

---

4. Bright, *Have You Heard of the Four Spiritual Laws?*

(your leaders) are never wrong. If we are, we'll never admit it. If we cause something that might look bad for us, it was some other country's fault. You citizens can't believe what you want—you can't be exposed to other views, so our version of reality is what you'll hear (no free press). Your religious views are forbidden. We, the state, are your gods. We'll tell you what's important and what to venerate.

Organizations can do the same. I think of the incident of the radical Islamic group Boko Haram, who exert their power in Nigeria and neighboring countries. In 2014 they kidnapped almost three hundred mostly Christian Nigerian school girls, between ages sixteen and eighteen, and tried to coerce them to be their wives, nearly starving them if they did not comply.[4] They also used them as bargaining chips for release of their comrades. The latest seizure (in 2021) involved 140 pupils.[5] They think coercion will get them what they want. Some radical religious groups think coercion is an acceptable way to gain converts. They try to force captives to vow allegiance to their God, and if they do, they have a new convert! Historically one can think of the causes of most (but not all) wars. Leaders can't get what they want through civilized means, and so they try to physically destroy enemies, seize their countries for their resources, or take them over just to expand their domain.

Economic organizations—companies—sometimes behave the same, worshipping being at the top of the heap. They try their best to get the market share of business, push competitors out by hook or crook, and underpay or poorly treat employees. It's all about the big S. During the last century, labor unions became more powerful and lobbied for the fair treatment and payment of employees. Strikes were frequently in the news. Much of this effort brought forth good results for employees, but sometimes the efforts bankrupted companies who could not realistically meet demands. Today the two battle back and forth to see who can get the most for their side. Treating our neighbor as ourselves is not even on the radar.

On the more personal level spousal abuse is also about the use of power to get what one wants. In other relationships, if power is too dangerous, there is always manipulation, such as blackmail—give me what I want and I'll give you what you want—or manipulating someone's emotional, financial, or relational weaknesses. Murder is an ultimate show of selfish power, taking a life because someone got in our way somehow.

---

4. Winsor and Bwala, "More Chibok Girls."
5. BBC News. "Nigeria Kidnap."

TEMPTATION

The James 1:14 quote earlier used the word "temptation," which means some sort of influence or nudge toward doing something that we know is wrong or to put big S on the throne. The difference between temptation and sin matters because we humans sometimes confuse the two. Some people believe they are constantly sinning because they regularly feel desires rise up, thinking the mere presence of an initial thought or feeling is sinful. Men see a beautiful woman and feel attracted; people see a sumptuous meal and want to splurge; those that come home from work tired wish their family would not put immediate demands on their time; we want to tell someone off in anger when he or she disappoints us repeatedly. However, these are manifestations of the influences of people or situations around us, our own desires, or even the devil working on our hearts; they are means of temptation and not sin itself. If the man above continues to gaze at a beautiful woman and then chooses to fantasize what she looks like naked and imagines having sex with her, then he has crossed over into lust and sin (see Matt 5:28). If the disappointed person lets go a flurry of angry words, disregarding more appropriate responses, he or she has likely sinned. In each case the critical point is what we do with the initial thought or feeling, many of which are involuntary. It is the next step that determines the holiness or sinfulness of our response. There is no need for guilt for feeling tempted; guilt rightly attaches only when we give in to the temptation.

Distinguishing the difference also encourages us. We can be encouraged that we can be as God asks us to be. What we should conclude is that we are in a spiritual battle and need to raise our shield and fight back. If that first involuntary thought or feeling is already a sin, then why fight the battle? We are doomed. But that is not the case. Those that respond to God's offer of power over sin as discussed in the next chapter have confidence they can overcome it. So let's see temptation for what it is and not give it more weight than it deserves.[6]

Conversely, we should not put ourselves in positions where we know we will be tempted. This just makes it harder to resist and shows that temptation may be stronger than we give it credit for. If persons are tempted by pornography, then they should put viewing controls on their computer. If one is tempted by alcohol, it is not wise to hang out with our drinking buddies. If we really want to avoid sin, then we should not be standing near the temptation fence while craning our necks over the edge to see how close we can get without going over. If this is the case, then we show we are not very

---

6. The train of thought for this section is taken from DeYoung, "Temptation Is Not the Same as Sin."

serious about avoiding sin. The apostle Paul instructed his younger pastoral apprentice, Timothy, to actually "flee" temptation: "Flee the evil desires of youth and pursue righteousness, faith, love and peace, along with those who call on the Lord out of a pure heart. Don't have anything to do with foolish and stupid arguments, because you know they produce quarrels" (2 Tim 2:22–23).

THE FALLOUT FROM HUMAN SIN[7]

One thing is clear—since we are all now "east of Eden" we do experience the *indirect* effects of Adam's sin. This means we do not enjoy Eden's protection and therefore experience toil in working the ground for food, extra pain in childbirth, and distorted marriage relationship tendencies. We develop from infancy with our physical and emotional desires dominating.[8] Our parents likely met our physical needs whenever we cried; we were tuned into our own needs and wants and were not required to think of others. Our creature comforts were satisfied before we developed a concept of the value of others and their needs/wants. When our wants conflicted with those of our parents or our brothers and sisters, our tendency was to meet ours first. That is the way human growth has been so far. This is not bad or evil; it is just the way life is. Moreover, some of us grew up in a family where there was a push toward looking after ourselves first. This is what we saw modeled, and we assumed this was the way life should operate. If we grew up in an altruistic family, life was better. We witnessed unselfish behavior more than not, and learned the importance of loving others.

No matter our family's persuasion, in family life and school we discovered others can be loving or unloving. For example, others sometimes made fun of us, and we sometimes made fun of them. If we were the recipient, we felt hurt and wronged. If we were the perpetrator, our conscience likely bothered us, and we felt guilty. On the other hand, if we saw others behave in an unselfish, loving way, we saw the benefits. If it was us, we frequently got respect or praise by helping others or doing what we knew pleased others, especially those in charge. This made us feel good; we sensed this is the way things ought to be. We are all witnesses that the people we rub shoulders with frequently influence us. Parents, siblings, friends, social institutions, and culture's effect on our decision-making is large—sometimes for

---

7. This section is largely from Christensen, *God, Adam, and You*, 135–41.

8. If Adam and Eve had been obedient, and in that state raised children, would our self-oriented physical and emotional desires described here have been less? Probably, but the answer is unknown.

good and sometimes not. The indirect effects of *negative* influences could be multiplied by many paragraphs and the effects seen in every person's life. These influences push us toward sin.

The biblical writers sometimes refer to this negative influence of who and what is around us as "the world." This is the current worldly system dominated by sin and can include culture, social systems, and in general the negative influence from others. This idea is clearest in the apostle John's writings. He warns his readers:

> Do not love the world or anything in the world. If anyone loves the world, love for the Father is not in them. For everything in the world—the lust of the flesh, the lust of the eyes, and the pride of life—comes not from the Father but from the world. The world and its desires pass away, but whoever does the will of God lives forever. (1 John 2:15–17)

John reminds us that this world is under the influence of the evil one, Satan (1 John 5:19). Therefore James says we should not be friends with it (Jas 4:4) or allow ourselves to be polluted by it (Jas 1:27). Its friends are enemies of God.

The Cost of Sin to God—A Story of Longsuffering

The following two stories combine together to illustrate the challenge God has when it comes to dealing with human sin. The first is a biblical story from the first book of the Bible, Genesis. It is the time of Noah.

> The Lord regretted that he had made human beings on the earth, and his heart was deeply troubled. So the Lord said, "I will wipe from the face of the earth the human race I have created—and with them the animals, the birds and the creatures that move along the ground—for I regret that I have made them." But Noah found favor in the eyes of the Lord. (Gen 6:6–8)

God had such high hopes for those in his image. He had given them everything they needed to prosper, to worship him, and to live peacefully with each other. What they did was to repeatedly do harm to themselves and their fellows. One can imagine what they did—extortion, adultery, taking advantage of the weak and poor, amassing wealth at the expense of others, lying, bribery; the list was likely long—and God had waited patiently for them to turn back to him. But they paid no attention; they were intent on self-destruction and on spurning God's goodness.

THE TURNING AWAY   43

The second story is from the modern-day experience of aviator Dean Harvey.[9] He tells his story, which I've adapted here:

As a thirty-year Navy man I used to fly a lot, mostly in an AD Skyraider. We had a four-man crew and I was the navigator. We left Naval Air Station San Diego on March 10, 1961, to participate in some war games over the Pacific. At four thousand feet our engine literally exploded and caught fire. Soon our pilot called back to us on the intercom, "Prepare to bail out." During those few minutes I remember being as scared as I have ever been. It was like my stomach came up in my throat, and there was no doubt I was going to die. As a Christian I was not afraid of death, but I was afraid of the physical pain or drowning in the ocean. We ditched in the ocean at high speed. Water came pouring through the fuselage, and as I looked around I was the only one still in the plane. I unbuckled my seatbelt and swam a short distance away, just in time to see the vertical stabilizer disappear under the water. Thankfully, I was rescued. In the hospital they looked me over, and all I had was a scratch on my cheek. It was a miracle. Fast forward now to 1983. I was teaching some classes at School of the Bible in Tyler, Texas. At lunch there was usually a lot of conversation, but today everyone was quiet. When I asked what was up I was told that a South Korean passenger jet had just been shot down by a Russian fighter. Many lives were lost, including a US Congressman. I watched the TV news that night and saw coverage of the incident. A camera focused on a small elderly woman aided by two husky Korean servicemen. Tears were streaming down her wrinkled face; she was waiting for a family member to arrive on that plane. As I watched, in my heart I heard God say, "Dean, what do you see?" I told God what I had just witnessed on the TV. He repeated the question. I was more specific this time, "I see a brokenhearted woman." God asked, "How did you feel when you first heard about this tragedy?" I said, "I was mad. I thought of the 269 people who as they were going down had the same fear I had during my plane crash. They knew in a few minutes they were going to die." (It actually took over twelve minutes for the plane to crash after being struck.) Then the Lord asked me, "What is the difference between you and this Korean lady?" It came to me, "I didn't love anyone on that plane." But someone she loved, whom she had come to the airport to meet, was permanently torn from her. Grief's emotional suffering is proportional to the level of intimacy and loss. I was then reminded of the Scripture from Genesis 6 and that God was sorry he had made humankind and he was grieved in his heart at their conduct. God was grieved because he loved these people he had made in his image, he was patient with them, especially those people who were "wicked and the

---

9. Harvey, *Ransom*, 16–19.

intent of their thoughts was only evil continually." He wanted to be intimate with them but they would not! What an incredibly high cost sin produces in the heart of the great loving God!

The Personal Consequences of Our Own Sin

The consequences for our own sins have been partially discussed above. Spiritual death is an obvious consequence; we are estranged from God and frequently from those around us. Isaiah illustrates this in his words to the Israelites in Isaiah 59:2: "But your iniquities have separated you from your God; your sins have hidden his face from you, so that he will not hear." Here are some other personal consequences from our own sin.

Shame and Guilt

The consequence of separation, estrangement, and death is certainly vertical (between us and God). Many consequences are horizontal (personal and social). For instance, like Adam and Eve, when our own sin looms in front of our minds, we seek to hide and cover it up (think fig leaves, Gen 3:7). This is internal shame and a sense of personal guilt. A frequent follow-up is blame—it's someone else's fault for what I did (see the blame game in Gen 3:12, 13.); this is social.

The guilt that follows sin was even inherent in some of the Hebrew "sin" words. For them, legal guilt is intricately tied in. James highlights this by declaring that he who offends God's law in one point is guilty of breaking all of it (Jas 2:10). Again, this kind of guilt is legal—it carries a moral debt to God. The sin and guilt offerings of the OT dealt with such things and restored fellowship with God and with those who were sinned against. In the NT those in Christ are justified or declared "not guilty" because of his gracious atonement.

We may think shame and guilt are of no value or are even harmful, but that conclusion would be premature. God designed us to experience guilt so we would be painfully aware that we had done something wrong, something that displeased him, something we were never designed to do. It's a wake-up call to repent,[10] to humbly come before God and ask for his forgiveness and

---

10. "Repent" is a biblical word that means to turn away from sin and toward God. It means we've changed our mind about the value of sin and the value of loving God. It frequently includes the ideas of regret and remorse for what we've done and also the idea of confession—we confess our wrongs to God and to those we have hurt.

for the ability to live differently. Guilt leads us to restore a broken relationship, and that's a good thing.

Restlessness and Trouble

Those who neglect God live agitated lives. All of us can sympathize with this feeling. Those who rebel against God are internally uncomfortable and bring this same unrest to those around them.[11] Isaiah says it so well: "But the wicked are like the tossing sea, which can not rest, whose waves cast up mire and mud. 'There is no peace,' says my God, 'for the wicked'" (Isa 57:20–21). This lack of peace leads to weariness, sorrow, and misery.[12] Adam and Eve's story has been discussed; they were banished from God's Garden and opened a Pandora's box that the rest of us have had to deal with ever since. In another situation, it was Jonah who brought trouble and calamity to himself, the sailors, and the ship he was on by refusing to preach to the city of Nineveh (Jon 1:8). Sin and betrayal tortured the soul of Judas, who finally hanged himself in his remorse for betraying Christ (Matt 27:3–5) and also tortured Peter, who denied knowing Jesus (Matt 26:69–75). We all bear self-inflicted wounds that scar our lives, leaving sin-marks to be healed. Most of our own stories also involve sins done against us. Sin surely brings pain and turmoil.

This general heading of "trouble" could be vastly expanded; it is a word that can encompass all the evil that results from sin. Personally, we can sin against our body (gluttony, sloth, any harmful drug usage, adultery) and irreparably harm our bodies, affecting quality and quantity of life, creating financial hardship, and distressing God's heart. If we lie, we frequently tune out our conscience, experience guilt, and harm our reputation when the lie is found out. Lies breed lack of trust from others and harm them when they act on our un-truths. Adultery does similar things—it deeply wounds a life-long bond, leads to guilt both real and false, breaks up families, frequently provokes financial hardship, jades children's respect for marriage, damages reputations, and so on. Spiritually, apathy or lukewarm-ness toward God lulls Christians to accept a substandard relationship with God and thwarts God's attempt to mature them. Prayers are ineffective, and desire for God wanes. Family, children, and others who observe them may be tempted to think this is the normal Christian life and be tempted to follow the pattern. All the while God is ready to spit such people out of his mouth (Rev 3:14–19)!

---

11. Erickson, *Christian Theology*, 594.
12. Erickson, *Christian Theology*, 595.

A Hardened Heart and Bondage

If we leave sin unchecked in our lives, we discover it becomes harder and harder to resist and easier and easier to succumb to its desires. If we eventually do wish to turn to God, the journey can be very difficult. How does a hard heart develop? The proverb that says "sow an act, reap a habit, sow a habit, reap a character, sow a character, reap a destiny" is an illustration of the same truth found in verses we have seen before: "But each person is tempted when they are dragged away by their own evil desire and enticed. Then, after desire has conceived, it gives birth to sin; and sin, when it is full-grown, gives birth to death" (Jas 1:14–15). A hard heart begins with the thought that whatever sin offers is better than what God does. Sin entices and promises to deliver what will satisfy, but its pleasures are fleeting and incomplete. The "having" is not near as good as the "wanting" or the "anticipating." Contentment and fulfillment seem just out of reach, so greater and greater sinning ensues, leading only to disillusionment and bondage. All the while sin has quietly calloused the heart; God's voice has become harder to hear, less important, and less relevant. It is no wonder, then, that the Bible's Greek words used to describe this hardness, *sklerynō*, *porōsis*, and *pachyno*, suggest something impenetrable, insensitive, blind, and unteachable. These mind states do not develop overnight, but are the result of habitually neglecting the conscience and the voice of God.[13] One is reminded of Charles Dickens' *A Christmas Carol*, where Jacob Marley's ghost staggers under the heavy chains hanging from his neck, forged by a lifetime of greed and indifference to the world. Marley fashioned each link himself, one by one, until he had forged a ponderous length. Learning his lesson too late, he now confronts Ebenezer Scrooge's own hard heart.

This pattern is not new. In the OT, God allowed the Israelites to divorce because their hearts had become hard (Matt 19:8). It was a concession to their unwillingness to love their mates. Israel's King Zedekiah hardened his heart (became "stiff-necked") toward the Lord. He wouldn't listen to Jeremiah the prophet, and as a result, the leaders, priests, and people defiled themselves with idols (2 Chr 36:11–14). All this occurred for Zedekiah between age twenty-one and thirty-two. You don't need to be old to have a hard heart! This hardness was also prevalent on a larger scale in the nation of Israel whom God and his servants called "stiff-necked" nineteen times! Therefore *they wouldn't listen* (remained in willful ignorance, 2 Kgs 17:14; Neh 9:29) and *forgot* the miracles God did for them (Neh 9:16–17).

---

13. Ritenbaugh, "What Sin Is," 6–7.

A NT Gospel story is similar. Though not meaning the same, it was "hard" for the rich man to enter the kingdom of heaven (Matt 19:23) because his heart was already filled with seemingly more important things—power, wealth, possessions, ease. It is difficult for Christ's words to break through an exterior that is so preoccupied. Likewise, Paul reminded the Ephesians that the hardness of gentiles'[14] hearts led to ignorance (Eph 4:17–19). Their "understanding was darkened" because there was a loss of sensitivity (apparently to what is right and wrong). This led to grosser forms of sexual impurity and greediness—a real downward spiral! Even today there are those who neglect God and therefore don't know anything about him. When asked they admit their ignorance, but when given the opportunity to know this God they are not interested! It is hard to appeal to them because they are happy in their ignorance. It often takes a crisis to break the crust of their heart and open a window of opportunity for God to shine his light in.

If left unchecked, sin can lead to eventual apostasy and hell. In the OT story Eli the priest's sons, Hophni and Phineas, had become so stubborn (They were called "scoundrels," 1 Sam 2:12) in not fulfilling their duties as priests that the only recourse was for God to kill them (1 Sam 2:25). Such was also the fate of Pharaoh. We see in the book of Exodus that he already had developed a hard heart when God hardened it further and used him to bring judgment on himself and the Egyptian nation (Exod 7–14). It appears there was then no more hope for Pharaoh; his only usefulness to God was as an instrument of judgment and as an object lesson for Israel of what not to become.

In the NT Paul warned the Romans about the sins of idolatrous gentiles whom he gave over to their sexual desires, homosexuality, greed, and many other vices (Rom 1:29–31). Without repentance they were surely headed for hell. The writer of Hebrews even warns Christians: "See to it, brothers and sisters, that none of you has a sinful, unbelieving heart that turns away from the living God. But encourage one another daily, as long as it is called 'Today,' so that none of you may be hardened by sin's deceitfulness" (Heb 3:12–13). He later warns that eternal destruction is not the fate of pagans only; Christians need to guard their hearts:

> It is impossible for those who have once been enlightened, who have tasted the heavenly gift, who have shared in the Holy Spirit, who have tasted the goodness of the word of God and the powers of the coming age and who have fallen away, to be brought back to repentance. To their loss they are crucifying the Son of God all over again and subjecting him to public disgrace. Land that drinks

---

14. A "gentile" is someone who is not a Jew.

> in the rain often falling on it and that produces a crop useful to those for whom it is farmed receives the blessing of God. But land that produces thorns and thistles is worthless and is in danger of being cursed. In the end it will be burned. (Heb 6:4–8)

Diversion and Indifference

It seems that we humans have an aversion to dwelling on the ideas of shame, guilt, the restlessness and trouble that sin brings, and the consciousness our hearts are becoming hard. That's understandable because they are surely unpleasant. If we don't deal with our guilt and restlessness in a constructive way, then the only option is to somehow cover it up or ignore it. That strategy is easy to see when one looks at how people who are not in a good relationship with God behave.

Two common but harmful coping strategies are diversion and indifference. These are intuitive if we consider how we behave in a relationship with a person we, for whatever reason, don't want to know or to whom we have done some harm. What do we do? First, we don't think about them much because we are not interested or the thoughts make us uncomfortable. Second, we just avoid them. We don't return their phone calls, we make excuses for rejecting invitations to be together, we don't frequent places they frequent, etc. If we are forced by circumstances we sometimes buck up the courage and tell them we just don't like them or don't care to be around them. In other words, please don't bother me!

These are the same strategies people tend to use with God. Blaise Pascal again has a timeless insight. Concerning diversion it's clear: "If our condition were truly happy we should not need to divert ourselves from thinking about it."[15] If one observes American culture we see we have plenty of diversion and amusement options that we can fill our time with. There's TV twenty-four hours a day, radio, cell phones, Facebook, anything you want to read or see on the internet, video games, chat rooms, books, sports, clubs, parties, gambling, being entertained, shopping, hobbies, using legal and illegal drugs, our jobs, keeping busy, and the list could go on. Some of these activities are necessary, and some help us recreate. But they can be harmful if used as a means of avoiding solitude, doing better things, thinking about our life's direction, or contemplating who God is and how we should relate to him and others. Do we do these things because they are necessary, like a job, or would we do something like a job anyway because it keeps our mind

---

15. Kreeft, *Christianity*, 169.

busy? A busy mind doesn't have to contemplate ultimate topics. For many free time is not for peace and rest but something to be filled with activity—peace, quiet, and rest just aren't that pleasant. Why isn't quiet pleasant for some? Pascal reminds us it is usually because of our wretchedness, our sin. It's because our relationships with God and others aren't right. He comments (boldface) and Peter Kreeft adds useful comments:

> **The only thing that consoles us for our miseries is diversion. And yet it is the greatest of our miseries. For it is that above all which prevents us thinking about ourselves and leads us imperceptibly to destruction. But for that we should be bored, and boredom would drive us to seek some more solid means of escape, but diversion passes our time and brings us imperceptibly to our death.**
>
> Diversion's greatest danger is that it acts like a sedative; it keeps us just content enough so that we don't make waves and seek a real cure. It deadens our spiritual nerves, it muffles our alarm system.
>
> A little respectable religion acts in the same way: as a mild dose of the infection, which builds up antibodies in us to shield us against the real thing. The Devil loves a little religion. He doesn't want us to be too bored and too miserable—yet.[16]

Another unhelpful and frequently sinful coping strategy is indifference. Some would say that hate is the opposite of love, and a person could make a good case for that conclusion. But an equally good case could be made that indifference, not caring one way or the other, is just as opposed to love. That indifferent attitude toward religion has been recently measured. Pew Research states that "Religious 'nones'—a shorthand we use to refer to people who self-identify as atheists or agnostics, as well as those who say their religion is 'nothing in particular'—now make up roughly 23 percent of the US adult population. This is a stark increase from 2007, the last time a similar Pew Research study was conducted, when 16 percent of Americans were 'nones.'"[17]

But is indifference harmful or sinful? It seems an inescapable conclusion that if love is commanded of us, which it is (think of the two Great Commandments). Peter Kreeft explains its danger:

> Diversion and indifference are the Devil's two most successful weapons against faith and salvation, the two widest roads to Hell in today's world. It is much harder for him to tempt us

---

16. Kreeft, *Christianity*, 186.
17. Lipka, "A Closer Look."

> with deliberate rebellion against God, for that uses two things that come from God: light and passion. Both can be twisted, but they are not the Devil's natural element. His natural elements are darkness and fog, not light; and sleep and death, not passion. Both diversion and indifference drain off passion and light—not only the light of faith but even the light of simple sanity and natural reason...
>
> Both diversion and indifference can be used for good—when the thing we are diverted from, or indifferent to, is bad for us. For instance, the Lamaze method of natural childbirth teaches the mother to divert herself from her labor pains by concentrating on breathing, like yoga. And drugs make us dull and indifferent to pain.
>
> But the only long-range solution to pain, whether physical or spiritual, is to listen to what it is telling us... Perpetual indifference is like shutting off the alarm clock and going back to sleep when the house you are in, which you have built upon the sand, is about to be washed away into the sea.[18]

God's promise is that we will find him if we seek him with all our heart. Pascal reminds us that seeking is necessary because God has intentionally revealed himself conditionally; he is findable by those who seek and not by those who do not. Since our souls are immortal, this seeking should be of the greatest importance and really the ultimate objective of our whole life. Pascal has great compassion for those who are in the midst of intense seeking after God but who have not yet found him. He is irritated and appalled by those who put forth little effort, who value their eternal souls to such a low degree, that they can not take the time or summon forth the courage to find the truth on such eternal matters.[19] To care is the prerequisite of all knowing and of experiencing all that is good. Kreeft comments on Pascal's Pensée 427:

> To care is even more important than to know, for it is the only way to know the most important thing about yourself, your soul, your identity, your purpose, your destiny and your immortality. If we are indifferent instead of seeking, we simply will not find, that is, we will not be saved. Hell is not populated mainly by passionate rebels but by nice, bland, indifferent, respectable people who simply never gave a damn.[20]

---

18. Kreeft, *Christianity*, 188–89.
19. Kreeft, *Christianity*, 188–91.
20. Kreeft, *Christianity*, 196.

We Can Lead Others toward Sin

As we have seen, human-to-human influence is very potent and includes all the people we rub shoulders with. Jesus especially warned his disciples about leading others away from him. He told them that "If anyone causes one of these little ones—those who believe in me—to stumble, it would be better for them to have a large millstone hung around their neck and to be drowned in the depths of the sea. Woe to the world because of the things that cause people to stumble! Such things must come, but woe to the person through whom they come!" (Matt 18:6–7). This influence started early in human history. Eve led Adam astray. Cain killed his brother Abel. Leaders, priests, and kings led Israel off target. Delilah instigated Samson's downfall. We ourselves may be guilty of nudging others toward sin, and we all likely can think of instances where others pushed us away from God and toward something evil. Many of us bear the marks of dysfunctional families and neighborhoods. Certainly we humans have great impact on each other and sometimes that impact is toward sin.

GREATNESS AND WRETCHEDNESS

The stories we have recited here are sad. They pain our hearts. There was such great potential for good but such a deep fall into selfishness. As we've seen, sometimes it is the fault of others. It is like looking at a young black boy, gifted with intellect and nimble hands, who is never given a chance to shine as a surgeon because he is too poor and too black.[21] Or, like a retired teacher, wizened by much training and life experience, is disqualified for work with young people because she is "just not what we're looking for" (in other words, too old). Sometimes it is our own fault. It is like a promising athlete, gifted with great physical skills, who throws away his opportunity by preferring late-night parties and sexual conquests (think Johnny Manziel). Or, it's like the mother who is skilled in leadership, who is so intent on making a name for herself in business, that she neglects her children and alienates her husband.[22] We sigh and think to ourselves, "What a waste." And so it is.

Our freedom to choose our own destiny gives us the power to choose which fork in the road we will take. Blaise Pascal called it the problem of

---

21. For the story behind this see Sargent, *Something the Lord Made*.
22. I think of the song "Cat's in the Cradle" by Harry Chapin. In the song it was the father. Both can be tempted to upend priorities.

"greatness and wretchedness."[23] We have already discussed some of the marvelous abilities and possibilities we all possess and have reviewed just a few examples of people who have used their gifts for ill. Pascal's emphasis is that great moral highs and lows can exist in the same person, and he declares that no other religion or philosophy can explain this paradox like Christianity can. Can they explain the life of David, who God said was "a man after mine own heart" (Acts 13:22) and who was chosen to be king over the nation of Israel? He was a courageous young man in the service of King Saul who, when other warriors would not rise to the challenge in the battle against the Philistines, stepped forward to kill the giant Goliath with a sling and a few stones. He later repeatedly spared the life of jealous and fearful King Saul, who tried to kill him on several occasions. When David did become king he, against convention, saved King Saul's crippled son, Mephibosheth, and made him part of his own household.[24] This same King David also desired to have Bathsheba, the wife of one of his soldiers, Uriah, so much that he sent him into the front lines of battle in hopes he would be killed. And Uriah was killed, and David married Bathsheba! When he had a child with Bathsheba, Nathan the prophet confronted him and told him God had judged him. God struck David's son with illness, and he soon after died. In other accounts we see the sons of David behaving badly, likely due at least in part to poor parenting and David's too-many concubines. In this dysfunctional family, "Absalom, the son of his third wife, murdered Amnon, David's firstborn, the son of his first wife, in revenge for Amnon raping Absalom's sister Tamar. Absalom later incited a violent rebellion against David and nearly displaced him as king. And even after David chose Solomon to succeed him, another son named Adonijah nearly took over the kingdom instead. Solomon ultimately had Adonijah executed."[25] What a story of greatness and wretchedness, all in one person! We can think of people in our own time who had altruistic attitudes and great gifts but were brought down by their sins. Politicians, financiers, and Christian leaders come to mind. The news is full of politicians, many very intelligent and charismatic, brought down by sexual scandal or financial sleight-of-hand. Wealthy businesspersons, given the gift to succeed in the financial world, break laws to line their own pockets and care little for the devastation of hard-working investors (Bernie Madoff comes to mind). Then there are gifted Christian leaders with successful ministries or churches brought

---

23. See a summary of Pascal's thoughts in Velarde, "Greatness and Wretchedness."

24. Most kings of David's time killed the sons of the previous monarchs to prevent these descendants from seeking the throne for themselves. This was usually done through assassination.

25. Smith, "Was It a Sin."

down by sexual affairs or misconduct—Jim Bakker, Jimmy Swaggart, Bill Gothard, Ted Haggard, Jerry Falwell Jr. and Becki Falwell, Bill Hybels, and Ravi Zacharias. Others committed fraud, such as Robert Tilton, or were too big in their own eyes, such as Mark Driscoll.

This is what sin can do in a life. The thing is, we all have the potential for both greatness and wretchedness, and God watches and spurs us on toward greatness.

SUMMARY

God's creation started out so well. There was a beautiful Garden, animals living together in harmony, and to top it off creatures made in his image. What a marvelous beginning! So, what in the world is God up to in allowing such a choice, *a choice either for or against him*? The answer is that creatures who can genuinely love must also be able to genuinely hate or be indifferent. There is no value in love if it were not so. Our first pair, Adam and Eve, likely did live for a while in harmony with God's plan, but the temptation to give in to unhealthy desires was also there. God wanted them to love him freely, and eventually they used that freedom to choose lesser things—fake knowledge, a satisfied hunger, and a pretty exterior package. We have all chosen similarly, with maybe different temptations that satisfy different desires. This is a large problem for God since this choosing the other, this sin, has brought separation, a broken creation, broken relationships, and death to his world. He could have left it at that and let humanity and the creation they spoiled continue on its course, from bad to worse. He could have started over with new image-bearers. He was even tempted to do that. He *did* destroy most of humankind with the flood, but preserved righteous Noah and his family:

> *The Lord saw how great the wickedness of the human race had become on the earth, and that every inclination of the thoughts of the human heart was only evil all the time. The Lord regretted that he had made human beings on the earth, and his heart was deeply troubled. So the Lord said, "I will wipe from the face of the earth the human race I have created—and with them the animals, the birds and the creatures that move along the ground—for I regret that I have made them." But Noah found favor in the eyes of the Lord.* (Gen 6:5–8)

He was later so angry with the idolatrous nation of Israel that he threatened to destroy them all and start over with Moses. He eventually relented as he remembered his covenant with Abraham and with them (Exod

32:9–14). Was this God's fault? Had he designed them so poorly that they could not obey? No, he had created them "very good." Was it Adam and Eve's fault—had they spoiled the whole world by introducing sin into it? They surely brought the evil influence of sin into the world, but no, each person is responsible for his/her own sin (Deut 24:16; Ezek 18; Eccl 7:29).

What would God do? These rebellious people could not undo their wrongs. Some of them didn't even want to. They were temporarily happy in their sins, and like us, they may have also succumbed to the temptations of diversion and indifference. He had to take the initiative if they were to be spared—and repaired. There had to be a way to bring them back into fellowship but to also honor the very good commands he had designed them to follow. After all, the commands came from his own nature and the nature of his creatures. How could he express his justice and mercy at the same time? Could it even be done?

3

Reconciliation

IF GOD WAS NOT loving, then the sin problem is easily solved—just judge all people for their transgressions and separate them from him forever. That would be the totally just[1] thing to do. However, there are other aspects to God's love that led him to another solution. Just as important as justice is God's mercy.[2] A totally merciful response would be to pardon them all no matter what they've done and regardless of their repentance or remorse for their sin. This would mean there would be no penalty or punishment. Neither of these extremes was ideal to God; therefore his path to a solution involved balancing these two equally valuable traits.

One thought is that there may be something these humans could do to restore this broken relationship. We reasonably think about our relationships with others. If one person does harm to another, there are steps to restore them to harmony. If the offender is remorseful, apologizes for his/her act, makes any amends or restitution that would repair any damage, and vows to not repeat the offense, then there is hope for restoration. The person hurt might then be receptive to those actions, believe the offender will not do this again, grant forgiveness, and restore the relationship. Given this human-to-human pattern, we might think God's response would be the same. But what about the damage done by the past sins? Does repentance

---

1. To be just in the biblical sense is to treat someone according to the pre-established standard of God's laws with their accompanying benefits for obedience and punishments for disobedience.
2. "Mercy" is frequently defined as undeserved favor.

and remorse undo the harm that was done? Does that adequately honor God's broken heart and broken commandments?

What if the offender repeats the sin, not just once, but time after time. He comes back remorseful and apologizes each time, but the pattern repeats. If the offended person forgives every time as before, is the relationship still "restored"? No, it isn't. If the offended party happens to be God, is *that* relationship "restored"? It doesn't seem so—there are still differences between behavior and God's commands—there has been no true change of mind and heart, and therefore there is no harmony. There is no love.

What could God possibly do to ensure respect for his good laws, now and in the future, show the great disappointment and anger God feels towards sin, and also transform the selfish human heart?

BALANCING JUSTICE AND MERCY[3]

The challenge of balancing justice and mercy is illustrated well in the story of Zaleucus, a seventh-century-BC ruler who was likely the first to write down laws in Greece. He lived in Locri, southern Italy. Zaleucus was especially concerned about adultery, which was running rampant. The wave of adultery was leading to the breakdown of the family and consequently threatening the region. He formulated a law that decreed that anyone committing adultery would be blinded by having both eyes put out. Naturally, the severity of the king's decree put considerable fear in the hearts of his subjects.

Alas, a short time passed, and a couple was caught in the very act of adultery. The male adulterer turned out to be Zaleucus' own son! When Zaleucus is informed of the arrest, the whole country was wondering, "How is he going to respond? Will he enforce the law by blinding his own son, or will he make an exception?" Naturally, as a father and as a private person, the king did not want to blind his own son, whom he loves. No father would want to do that. But on the other hand, there was the good of the city to consider. He was not merely a private person; he was a public official. He was a lawgiver who had the responsibility of enforcing the law. What would happen if he didn't enforce the law? People would lose respect for the law and continue to commit adultery. People would rightfully reason, "The lawgiver doesn't take his own decree seriously. If his son can get away with breaking the law, perhaps we can also."

He faced a dilemma. Either way he went, he would lose something valuable. If he was strictly just and went stringently according to the law, then mercy would suffer. On the other hand, if he was to unilaterally pardon,

---

3. This is an edited description of the story of Zaleucus from Shawny, "True Story."

justice would suffer. He was in a quandary. The king pondered his situation for a few days and finally called his son to stand before him. Zaleucus took a hot burning coal, and he pressed it against one of his son's eyes. Next, he pressed a second coal against his own eye. He burned out one of his own eyes!

What had been accomplished? He had made atonement. He came up with a substitute for the penalty of the law. He had personally suffered in his son's place. He believed this substitution would just as successfully accomplish the ends of the law as if he had totally blinded his son. What was the end of law? It was to uphold public justice, to promote the highest good of all, for both leaders and subjects.

What would be the reaction every time the people saw their one-eyed lawgiver and his one-eyed son? They were going to be reminded that this was a leader that took the law seriously. You can not break the law with impunity. So his action was going to promote lawfulness. Something else had been gained that would not have been secured had he completely blinded his son. The people learned their leader not only valued justice but also compassion: "What a loving and self-sacrificing leader we have! One who put out one of his own eyes for his son."

GOD'S DILEMMA

God's dilemma, then, like Zaleucus's, is to try to satisfy the equally appropriate demands of his justice and mercy. How can he show humans the reverential respect they should have for his laws—laws made for their good—without having them suffer the negative consequences of disobedience? As we've discussed, the consequences for any act reveal the severity of harm done. Sin is so disruptive to God's governing of us that death is the just result. Paul noted that the "wages of sin is death" (Rom 3:23). We've earned it. Is there any way to spare his creatures the death they deserve while simultaneously upholding the rightness and respect his laws deserve, that he himself deserves? From the human side *there is nothing they can do to "undo" the sin and the harm.* It is now past; the damage is done. Repentance and remorse are helpful but inadequate. The only possible solution, then, must come from God's side—and God does make the first move, the offended coming to the offenders and offering a way back. He begins his redemptive plan with Abraham.

THE ABRAHAMIC AND MOSAIC COVENANTS

The first redemptive covenant[4] God made was with Abram (later called Abraham) and is therefore called the Abrahamic covenant. God promised to bless Abraham, multiply his descendants into a great nation, and then give them a homeland. This would be a foundation through which God would bless the whole world (Gen 12:1–4). The continuation of God's covenant to Abraham was his covenant with the nation of Israel with Moses as God's chosen leader (the Mosaic covenant). God chose this small nation not because they were great but because he loved them and to keep his promise to their forefathers (Deut 7:6–8). They were to be a "kingdom of priests and a holy nation" (Exod 19:6) and a witness to the world of what living for God looked like. This is the beginning of redeeming the world.

However, the world would only know Israel was a divine entity powered by God if they lived like they were connected to him. To help them fulfill this commission God gave Israel special commandments and rules to live by—both as individuals and as a nation. He gave them the two Great Commandments about love toward him and others. He made these two more specific when he gave them his Ten Commandments when Moses received them engraved on tablets of stone at Mount Sinai. These are very general, and further detail was needed to help them as a nation to live a life pleasing to God. God saw fit to give Israel such detail in its laws, decrees, and statutes.[5] Though some are not valid for today, many principles and some specifics still apply.

To give us a bigger picture, John Gammie notes that God's call to law-keeping and holiness for Israel was responded to in three different but complementary ways by their priests, prophets, and sages. The priests

---

4. A covenant is a voluntary agreement between two parties in which each makes promises to fulfill certain obligations. Most of the biblical covenants have God making promises, and the covenant will not come to a satisfactory fulfillment unless humans also fulfill their promises. God has always fulfilled his promises, but humanity has not. Some of the covenants are not of a redemptive nature and are not discussed here. We are only looking at the ones that include the redemption of humankind as an essential part of their purpose.

5. God gave Israel a series of laws, statutes, and decrees so they could live as he intended and be a witness to the surrounding nations. For one, there were instructions on how to properly build and set up the tabernacle, their portable place of worship (Exod 25–40). God further delineated five main offerings (Lev 1–7), the priests' duties (Lev 8–10, 21–22), dietary rules for clean and unclean animals, purifications and cleansings (Lev 11–15), the Day of Atonement actions (Lev 16), annual festivals (Lev 23), miscellaneous rules (Lev 24–25), and rules for holy living in the land (Exod 20–23; Lev 17–20). The following section about Israel's priests, prophets, and sages is adapted from Christensen, *God, Adam, and You*, 205–08.

understood holiness to be separation or purification from what is unclean.[6] These are examples of God's call to be separate:

1. Abstaining from daily work on the Sabbath in order to honor God.
2. Worshipping only one God and not the gods of their neighbors.
3. Not intermarrying with neighboring peoples who worshipped false gods.
4. Establishing national boundaries.
5. Not eating blood or any unclean animal.
6. Obeying special dietary and sanitary restrictions that were different from their neighbors.
7. Observing many cleansing rituals to address physical and spiritual contamination.
8. Following specific religious rites, sacrifices, feasts, and modes of worship dedicated solely to God.
9. Following specific ethical principles, laws, and punishments when interacting among themselves, with foreign individuals, and with other nations. Topics included general morality, sex, finances, charity, fairness, interacting with the poor and the foreigner, and judicial propriety (see Lev 17–26, frequently called the "Holiness Code").

The priests knew that the ritual and ethical aspects were inseparable and complementary, and both were part of what it meant to be holy unto the Lord. For example, the priests supervised the various sin offerings (burnt, sin, guilt) and the Day of Atonement. They helped Israel as individuals and as a nation to purge and cleanse themselves from sin.[7]

The prophets of Israel understood all this as well, but they emphasized the moral more than the ritual aspect of holiness. They saw how Israel was turning away from God, and God used them to call Israel back to himself and to following his laws. For example, in Ezekiel 18 the priest-prophet Ezekiel commended many of the same moral acts described in Job 31 (sexual purity, fairness to servants, generosity to widows/orphans/the poor, trust in God and not wealth, no gloating over enemies' misfortune, being transparent about personal sins), the Ten Commandments, and Psalm 15 (the holy are truthful, do not slander, honor the good, honor promises, and reject usury

---

6. Gammie, *Holiness in Israel*, 2, 9.
7. Gammie, *Holiness in Israel*, 34, 39, 43–44.

and bribes).[8] The prophet Isaiah commanded the people to stop bringing meaningless offerings and sacrifices because their hearts were unclean (Isa 1:13–16) and put the spotlight on Israel's failure to provide social and legal justice for the powerless and poor (Isa 1:16–17, 27). This meant integrity was especially needed in the king and other rulers, but such qualities were sadly lacking (Isa 1:23; 11:3–4; 32:5–7).[9]

The theme of social justice was significant since Israel's leaders sometimes took advantage of the poor or weak. The prophets Amos and Micah addressed this. Amos called for justice in the courts for all, fair taxes for the poor, no bribe-taking, and a destruction of idols or God's judgment would fall (Amos 5). Micah decried the robbery of wealthy landowners, false prophets, unjust leaders, cheating grain dealers, judges who took bribes, and disloyal family members (Mic 2–3). To these specific ills Micah concludes,

> He has shown you, O mortal, what is good. And what does the Lord require of you? To act justly and to love mercy and to walk humbly with your God. (Mic 6:8)

Israel's sages and wisdom literature also promoted ethical purity and holiness, especially on the individual level. Two examples have already been cited—Job testified to the good things he has consistently done in his life that equate with the holiness God desires in his people (Job 31). David, in Psalm 15, described the behavior of one who can dwell in God's sacred tent and live on his holy mountain. He even testified to his own pattern of following God's ways, obedience, and relying on his faithfulness (Ps 26).[10]

For Israel, being holy is the proper response to God's holy character. God's command to be holy is to "be what you already are" and what he is. They were to act out in practice (the law) what God has already made them (a holy people); they were to live out their identity. By doing this they truly represented him and would be a light to the nations around them. And some individuals from neighboring nations did join Israel. People the Bible writers call "aliens" or "foreigners" could become part of the nation (Exod 12:48; Acts 2:10; 6:5; 13:43). A prominent individual comes to mind who did—Ruth, a Moabite, whose story is told in the OT book by her name.

---

8. Gammie, *Holiness in Israel*, 51.
9. Gammie, *Holiness in Israel*, 71–2, 83.
10. Gammie, *Holiness in Israel*, 149.

Mosaic Covenant Sacrifices

But what if, just like for Zaleucus and his son, an Israelite or an alien sinned by breaking one of the various laws God had instituted? This is where the sacrifices came in. Some sins could be covered (atoned for[11]) and forgiven through offering a blood sacrifice[12] (goat, cow), or for the poor a bird or fine flour. These were called "sin and guilt offerings" and were meant to cover mostly unintentional sins (sins done in ignorance, Num 15:22–36). If a person unknowingly broke a ceremonial law, for example, she needed to offer a sacrifice. Israelites were supposed to know the laws, so there was no excuse. The sacrifice reinstated them into fellowship with God, and they could move on and hopefully not repeat the same offense. There were a few instances where sins done intentionally could be forgiven. Leviticus 6 states that if someone lies to/about or cheats his neighbor (swears falsely or perjures himself) he must sacrifice a ram and make total restitution plus one fifth more; this is a guilt offering (Lev 6:1–7). This type of sin is envisioned by the eighth and ninth of God's Ten Commandments (do not steal, do not bear false witness).

However, death or exile was the punishment for breaking many of the Ten Commandments (Lev 20) and other intentional sins. There were no sacrifices a person could bring to atone for those intentional sins. The only recourse was the Day of Atonement (Yom Kippur), which occurred once per year. On this day the high priest would enter the holy of holies in the tabernacle[13] and sprinkle blood from bulls and rams on the mercy seat of the ark of the covenant[14] to atone for the sins of him and his family, to purify

---

11. To atone is to make "at one." It is to do what is necessary to restore a broken relationship. In the case of Israel it was to offer animal sacrifices as a substitute, giving a life for a life, so Israelites would be spared the death their sin deserved.

12. A blood sacrifice represented the giving of one life in place of another. Blood represented the life in the animal. Leviticus 17:11 says, "For the life of a creature is in the blood, and I have given it to you to make atonement for yourselves on the altar; it is the blood that makes atonement for one's life." Since the penalty of sin was death, this is why the blood sacrifice was required.

13. The tabernacle was the portable place of worship for the Israelites. God commanded how it was to be built and all the specific items and places it was to contain. When the Israelites moved, the tabernacle was disassembled and moved with them, to be reassembled when they had set up a new camp. For a more thorough description of it and the items it contained see Vision Video, "The Tabernacle," for a video presentation.

14. The ark of the covenant was a gold-plated acacia wood box that represented God's presence with the people of Israel. It housed the two Ten Commandments tablets, Aaron's rod that budded, and a golden jar of manna (food) that God fed Israel with during their wanderings in the Sinai desert. The cover contained two winged cherubim; this cover was called the mercy seat, where blood was sprinkled during the yearly Day

the altar and the tabernacle areas around the holy of holies, and to atone for the sins of the people. Specifically, the first goat was sacrificed as a sin offering on behalf of the people "because of the uncleanness and rebellion of the Israelites, whatever their sins have been" (Num 16:16). Next, the high priest took a second goat, laid his hands on its head, and confessed over it all the wickedness, rebellion, and sins of the Israelites. He then sent it out into the wilderness with someone guiding it out of the Israelite camp. The sins of Israel were therefore taken out away from them to a solitary place, never to return. This symbolized the removal of sin and its guilt from the camp of Israel. God had removed it from their midst; he had cleansed them of their sins (Num 16:30).

Substitution is a key concept implied in the sacrifices for unintentional and intentional sin. The whole point is for the sinner to avoid the just punishment of the law. The person deserved to face the consequences, but God wanted to make a way for sins to be removed. The sacrifices did this, but they would be ineffective if the sinner was not humble, contrite, and repentant. King David realized this after his sin with Bathsheba and Uriah. Psalm 51 is likely a psalm written after this sin, and he says to God:

> *You do not delight in sacrifice, or I would bring it; you do not take pleasure in burnt offerings. My sacrifice, O God, is a broken spirit; a broken and contrite heart you, God, will not despise.* (Ps 51:16–17)

Other Scriptures reveal the same thing about God's attitude toward sacrifices if they are not accompanied with sorrow for sin and repentance:

> *Does the Lord delight in burnt offerings and sacrifices as much as in obeying the Lord? To obey is better than sacrifice, and to heed is better than the fat of rams.* (1 Sam 15:22)

> *For I desire mercy, not sacrifice, and acknowledgment of God rather than burnt offerings.* (Hos 6:6)

God seems to describe a third category of sin that is especially heinous. It is sin that is "high-handed," or defiant towards God. God says, "But anyone who sins defiantly . . . blasphemes the Lord, and that person must be cut off from his people. Because he has despised the Lord's word and broken his commands, that person must surely be cut off; his guilt remains on him" (Num 15:30–31). These sins were "I don't care what God says, I'm going to do this anyway!"-type sins; they were unremorseful. There was no sacrifice that could cover such a sin, and God would not tolerate such blatant disobedience. It reflected poorly on the whole nation since Israel was to be God's

---

of Atonement sacrifices to atone for Israel's sins.

witness and a spiritual light to the whole world during that time. Exile was the only appropriate penalty.

So, has God balanced justice and mercy with these covenants? Yes, he has allowed unintentional and intentional sins to be forgiven if a substitute for the penalty of the law is provided—an animal can be sacrificed in place of the offender. But there are hints in the OT books that this covenant was a temporary solution for sin.

The Mosaic covenant was confirmed about five hundred years later when God made a covenant with the then-king of Israel, David. God blessed David and allowed his son, Solomon, to build the great temple[15] in Jerusalem that would replace their portable tabernacle. Here was the center of worship for Israel where the sacrifices were offered, where the ark of the covenant was housed, the Day of Atonement occurred, and where prayers and sacrifices were offered daily to God.

THE NEW COVENANT

There are signs in the OT that the Mosaic covenant was not the final solution to the problem of human sin and to a harmonious relationship with God. There was to come a "new covenant" that would be the fulfillment and climax of previous redemptive covenants and the promises made to Abraham, Moses, and David. Many Bibles headline the new covenant books with the words "New Testament," which have the same meaning. This New Testament will have better promises and offer the most complete salvation this side of heaven.

Two prophets, who lived about 250–300 years after David, especially mention this new covenant. Jeremiah prophesied:

> "The time is coming" declares the Lord, "when I will make a new covenant with the house of Israel and with the house of Judah. It will not be like the covenant I made with their forefathers when I took them by the hand to lead them out of Egypt, because they broke my covenant though I was a husband to them," declares the Lord.
>
> "This is the covenant I will make with the house of Israel after that time," declares the Lord. "I will put my law in their minds and write it on their hearts. I will be their God and they will be my people. No longer will a man teach his neighbor, or a man his brother, saying, 'Know the Lord,' because they will all know me, from the least of them to the greatest," declares the Lord. "For I will

---

15. For a more thorough video presentation of the temple and the function of its various parts, see Messages of Christ, "Solomon's Temple Explained."

forgive their wickedness and will remember their sins no more." (Jer 31:31–34)

Isaiah later mentions that this covenant will include gentiles and describes the person who will inaugurate it, who he calls a servant. He says, "I will also make you a light for the Gentiles, that you may bring my salvation to the ends of the earth" (Isa 49:6). Isaiah gives the clearest and most vivid description of this servant, who would be the coming Savior or Messiah ("Anointed One"):

He grew up before him like a tender shoot, and like a root out of dry ground. He had no beauty or majesty to attract us to him, nothing in his appearance that we should desire him. He was despised and rejected by mankind, a man of suffering, and familiar with pain. Like one from whom people hide their faces he was despised, and we held him in low esteem. Surely he took up our pain and bore our suffering, yet we considered him punished by God, stricken by him, and afflicted. But he was pierced for our transgressions, he was crushed for our iniquities; the punishment that brought us peace was on him, and by his wounds we are healed. We all, like sheep, have gone astray, each of us has turned to our own way; and the Lord has laid on him the iniquity of us all.

He was oppressed and afflicted, yet he did not open his mouth; he was led like a lamb to the slaughter, and as a sheep before its shearers is silent, so he did not open his mouth. By oppression and judgment he was taken away. Yet who of his generation protested? For he was cut off from the land of the living; for the transgression of my people he was punished. He was assigned a grave with the wicked, and with the rich in his death, though he had done no violence, nor was any deceit in his mouth.

Yet it was the Lord's will to crush him and cause him to suffer, and though the Lord makes his life an offering for sin, he will see his offspring and prolong his days, and the will of the Lord will prosper in his hand. After he has suffered, he will see the light of life and be satisfied; by his knowledge my righteous servant will justify many, and he will bear their iniquities. Therefore I will give him a portion among the great, and he will divide the spoils with the strong, because he poured out his life unto death, and was numbered with the transgressors. For he bore the sin of many, and made intercession for the transgressors. (Isa 53:2–12)

Isaiah further states that this "Branch" (a leader) would arise from David's lineage (Jer 23:5–6) and sit on his throne forever. Isaiah prophesies:

> *For to us a child is born, unto us a son is given, and the government will be on his shoulders. And he will be called Wonderful Counselor, Mighty God, Everlasting Father, Prince of Peace. Of the greatness of his government and peace there will be no end. He will reign on David's throne and over his kingdom, establishing and upholding it with justice and righteousness from that time on and forever. The zeal of the Lord Almighty will accomplish this.* (Isa 9:6–7; see also Ezek 37:24–28)

A thousand years later the angel spoke to Jesus' mother, Mary, when she was pregnant with him, and comforted her with similar words from 2 Samuel 7:16, which proclaim Jesus as the "Son of the Most High" who will sit on David's throne and whose reign and kingdom will never end (Luke 1:31–33). This King would inaugurate the new covenant God would make between himself and humankind.

Jesus and the OT Sacrifices

Jesus, then, the second person of the Trinity, and the Father's Son, is the Trinity's final solution to restoring humanity to themselves. Let's look at how this new covenant is better. One obvious feature of the OT is that sacrifices had to be made regularly by the priests to atone for sin. In the NT Jesus acts as the high priest but also as the sacrifice itself—he offers himself willingly once for the sin of the whole world! There is no need to repeat this ultimate sacrifice. No more need for the thousands of animals to suffer death and give their lives for the sins of human transgressors. Further, the priests had to make atonement for their own sin. Jesus is sinless and does not need to make any sacrifice for himself. Does that mean he can't sympathize with us like a human priest would? No. The writer of Hebrews tells us,

> *For this reason he had to be made like his brothers in every way, in order that he may become a merciful and faithful high priest in the service of God, and that he might make atonement for the sins of the people. Because he himself suffered when he was tempted, he is able to help those who are being tempted.* (Heb 2:17–18)

Suffering

This suffering was clearly described for us in the text of Isaiah 53. The servant would suffer at the hands of humankind, be despised and rejected. All this and he was innocent of any wrongdoing. Just like a sacrificed animal had to be perfect with no blemishes, so was the Son of God. And just like the bull or ram must die, life for life, so did the Son of God die in our place. The animal had no choice in the matter but the Savior did. He gave his life willingly:

> *I am the good shepherd; I know my sheep and my sheep know me—just as the Father knows me and I know the Father—and I lay down my life for the sheep . . . The reason my Father loves me is that I lay down my life—only to take it up again. No one takes it from me, but I lay it down of my own accord. I have authority to lay it down and authority to take it up again. This command I received from my Father.* (John 10:14–18)

The animal's suffering was also unknowing. It did not know why it was being killed. Jesus knew why. So beyond the extreme physical pain of a six-hour crucifixion there was the bearing of all the sins of humanity on his person. The suffering even began before, in the Garden of Gethsemane. While praying to his Father in heaven he became sorrowful and troubled. He said to his disciples before he began to pray, "My soul is overwhelmed with sorrow to the point of death" (Matt 26:38).

> Interestingly, "Gethsemane" means olive press. Near the garden was an olive grove, and it was probably in this garden that the olive oil was pressed out of the olives. It is here that Jesus prays for God to let this cup pass from Him. He prays so fervently, and is in such deep anguish, that drops of blood came out of His skin. He was being pressed like an olive. Physicians tell us that this is entirely possible when a person is under extreme amounts of stress and pressure.
>
> Though we can never know the spiritual agony that Jesus experienced on the cross, we see hints of it in what He says. For example, His fifth statement from the cross is "My God, My God, Why have you forsaken me?" Jesus, as the second person of the Trinity, has had constant fellowship with God the Father for all eternity. What must it have been like for Him now to have that relationship severed and broken? **What must it have felt like for Jesus when our sin separated Him from God?** . . .
>
> Imagine now being Jesus, never having sinned, never having known the pain and fear of guilt, never having felt hate or lust, now having the torrential flood of all the sins of the whole world placed upon Him in a few short hours. Every bad thought that has ever been thought, every adulterous affair, every hateful word, every act of theft or bribery, every whisper of gossip, every murder, every profanity, every act of disloyalty to wife, husband,

or boss, every disobedient act of children toward their mother, father, or teacher—all sin, of all the world, of all time was placed on Jesus Christ all at once.

Jesus took it all. He who had never experienced the pain of sin, took it all at once in a torrential downpour. It was beyond anything we can describe or understand.[16]

Blameless and Perfect

God required that the OT sacrificial animals be spotless, with no defects, and completely healthy. This symbolized the Israelites giving their best because sin was a serious breach in the relationship. No weak, diseased, or damaged animal that was of lesser worth to a family fully represented their best. This physical perfection is expressed in the person of Jesus, who lived a sinless life and always did what pleased his Father (Heb 4:15; Matt 17:5; John 8:29). His perfection was spiritual and relational. If he had somehow not been perfect he would have been under the same condemnation of the law that the Israelites had been and he would have been disqualified from being a sacrifice.

Why a New Covenant?

The question sometimes arises as to why God even began with the Mosaic covenant and why he didn't just fulfill his covenant with Abraham by sending his son in the beginning. Some speculate that the Mosaic covenant was needed as a spiritual preparation before people would understand God actually sending his son to atone for the sins of the world. The bottom line is that we do not know, but what we do know is that the new covenant was God's ultimate solution to bridging a relationship with his creation. The book of Hebrews clarifies the necessity of a new covenant. The writer states that the OT law and sacrifices were never meant to be and didn't have the power to be real solutions for sin; they were shadows of the real thing! The real atonement and forgiveness was only accomplished through the sacrifice of God's only son. As we said before, he acted not only as the high priest would on sinners' behalf, but as the sacrifice itself! The following passage is long (so don't skip it!) and is very clear on how Jesus completely fulfills his Father's purpose in taking away our sins and making us holy, something the Mosaic covenant could not do:

---

16. Myers, "Crucifixion."

But when Christ came as high priest of the good things that are now already here, he went through the greater and more perfect tabernacle that is not made with human hands, that is to say, is not a part of this creation. He did not enter by means of the blood of goats and calves; but he entered the Most Holy Place once for all by his own blood, thus obtaining eternal redemption. The blood of goats and bulls and the ashes of a heifer sprinkled on those who are ceremonially unclean sanctify them so that they are outwardly clean. How much more, then, will the blood of Christ, who through the eternal Spirit offered himself unblemished to God, cleanse our consciences from acts that lead to death, so that we may serve the living God!

For this reason Christ is the mediator of a new covenant, that those who are called may receive the promised eternal inheritance—now that he has died as a ransom to set them free from the sins committed under the first covenant.

In the case of a will, it is necessary to prove the death of the one who made it, because a will is in force only when somebody has died; it never takes effect while the one who made it is living. This is why even the first covenant was not put into effect without blood. When Moses had proclaimed every command of the law to all the people, he took the blood of calves, together with water, scarlet wool and branches of hyssop, and sprinkled the scroll and all the people. He said, "This is the blood of the covenant, which God has commanded you to keep." In the same way, he sprinkled with the blood both the tabernacle and everything used in its ceremonies. In fact, the law requires that nearly everything be cleansed with blood, and without the shedding of blood there is no forgiveness.

It was necessary, then, for the copies of the heavenly things to be purified with these sacrifices, but the heavenly things themselves with better sacrifices than these. For Christ did not enter a sanctuary made with human hands that was only a copy of the true one; he entered heaven itself, now to appear for us in God's presence. Nor did he enter heaven to offer himself again and again, the way the high priest enters the Most Holy Place every year with blood that is not his own. Otherwise Christ would have had to suffer many times since the creation of the world. But he has appeared once for all at the culmination of the ages to do away with sin by the sacrifice of himself. Just as people are destined to die once, and after that to face judgment, so Christ was sacrificed once to take away the sins of many; and he will appear a second time, not to bear sin, but to bring salvation to those who are waiting for him.

> *The law is only a shadow of the good things that are coming—not the realities themselves. For this reason it can never, by the same sacrifices repeated endlessly year after year, make perfect those who draw near to worship. Otherwise, would they not have stopped being offered? For the worshipers would have been cleansed once for all, and would no longer have felt guilty for their sins. But those sacrifices are an annual reminder of sins. It is impossible for the blood of bulls and goats to take away sins.*
>
> *Therefore, when Christ came into the world, he said:*
> *"Sacrifice and offering you did not desire,*
>   *but a body you prepared for me;*
> *with burnt offerings and sin offerings*
>   *you were not pleased.*
> *Then I said, 'Here I am—it is written about me in the scroll—*
>   *I have come to do your will, my God.'"*
>
> *First he said, "Sacrifices and offerings, burnt offerings and sin offerings you did not desire, nor were you pleased with them"—though they were offered in accordance with the law. Then he said, "Here I am, I have come to do your will." He sets aside the first to establish the second. And by that will, we have been made holy through the sacrifice of the body of Jesus Christ once for all.*
>
> *Day after day every priest stands and performs his religious duties; again and again he offers the same sacrifices, which can never take away sins. But when this priest had offered for all time one sacrifice for sins, he sat down at the right hand of God, and since that time he waits for his enemies to be made his footstool. For by one sacrifice he has made perfect forever those who are being made holy.* (Heb 9:11—10:14)

Forgiveness, Transformation, and the Holy Spirit

The above passage from Hebrews highlights important points that make the new covenant necessary. Forgiveness is a major point, as are also "cleansing the conscience, making perfect, and making holy." God not only wants to forgive us for our sins but to make us more like himself. It is not that holiness was not expected of the Israelites—it was. In Leviticus God told them to be holy for he is holy (Lev 19:2; 20:26). God commanded them to obey the Ten Commandments and all the other individual, ceremonial, and national laws. He never hinted they could not do so. Moses agreed with God, saying that the Israelites were eminently able to do all that God commanded (Deut 30:11–14). Even from the beginning, before the Mosaic covenant, it had always been faith or trust in God that pleased him, and this is rooted in love and leads naturally to obedience. The apostle James clarifies this for Jews that have now become Christians:

> Was not our father Abraham considered righteous for what he did when he offered his son Isaac on the altar? You see that his faith and his actions were working together, and his faith was made complete by what he did. And the scripture was fulfilled that says, "Abraham believed God, and it was credited to him as righteousness," and he was called God's friend. You see that a person is considered righteous by what they do and not by faith alone.
> In the same way, was not even Rahab the prostitute considered righteous for what she did when she gave lodging to the spies and sent them off in a different direction? As the body without the spirit is dead, so faith without deeds is dead. (James 2:21–24)

To make sure *Christians* do not forget, the apostle Peter repeats the call to holiness, reminding new believers that God has called them to be self-controlled, to cast off the evil desires they once obeyed, and to look forward to the return of Jesus at his second coming. They are to be holy because God is holy (1 Pet 1:13–16, quoting Lev 19:2).

But there is a new power under the new covenant. The writer of Hebrews talks about the inner cleansing of the conscience, being made perfect or complete, and being holy. There is a new freedom to be all that God has called us to be. This was foretold in the OT book of Jeremiah (Jer 31:31–34), a passage we have already read. God will put his law in their minds and write it on their hearts. We will be able to know God in a deeper way. This freedom seems to be directly related to another new feature—the Holy Spirit will now actually *indwell* Christians. In the OT the Holy Spirit came on individuals temporarily for a certain task or a certain purpose, but never as a lifelong indwelling presence. Now he will take up residence in those who love him. John the Baptist, the forerunner who announced Jesus' coming into the world, proclaimed that Jesus would baptize his followers with the Holy Spirit (Matt 3:11). The apostle John records Jesus' own declaration:

> On the last and greatest day of the festival, Jesus stood and said in a loud voice, "Let anyone who is thirsty come to me and drink. Whoever believes in me, as Scripture has said, rivers of living water will flow from within them." By this he meant the Spirit, whom those who believed in him were later to receive. Up to that time the Spirit had not been given, since Jesus had not yet been glorified. (John 7:37–39)

The apostle Paul reminds the believers in Corinth:

> *Do you not know that your bodies are temples of the Holy Spirit, who is in you, whom you have received from God? You are not your own.* (1 Cor 6:19)

It is the Holy Spirit who helps believers to do all that God asks of them. The apostle John calls him the "Comforter" or "Counselor" who will be with and in Christians all their days (John 16). This infilling or baptizing with the Holy Spirit began for NT believers at the Feast of Pentecost, soon after Jesus was resurrected into heaven (Acts 2), and continues to this day for all who believe.

Gentiles Included

During all of God's dealing with Abraham through the time of Jesus, God had dealt directly with the Jews, the people of Israel, as an intermediator between himself and those who were not Jews (gentiles). God has always loved gentiles, but has related to them in this way during the Abrahamic and Mosaic covenants. Anyone who lived before Abraham in history or who was not acquainted with the nation of Israel (many people) will be looked at by God in a very fair way—he will look at what was in their hearts. Paul makes this clear in his letter to the Romans. He is writing to Jews and others who were looking down on people who they considered sinful or who were gentiles:

> *God "will repay each person according to what they have done." To those who by persistence in doing good seek glory, honor and immortality, he will give eternal life. But for those who are self-seeking and who reject the truth and follow evil, there will be wrath and anger. There will be trouble and distress for every human being who does evil: first for the Jew, then for the Gentile; but glory, honor and peace for everyone who does good: first for the Jew, then for the Gentile. For God does not show favoritism.*
>
> *All who sin apart from the law will also perish apart from the law, and all who sin under the law will be judged by the law. For it is not those who hear the law who are righteous in God's sight, but it is those who obey the law who will be declared righteous. (Indeed, when Gentiles, who do not have the law, do by nature things required by the law, they are a law for themselves, even though they do not have the law. They show that the requirements of the law are written on their hearts, their consciences also bearing witness, and their thoughts sometimes accusing them and at other times even defending them.) This will take place on the*

> day when God judges people's secrets through Jesus Christ, as my gospel declares.[17] (Rom 2:6–16)

Now God, in the new covenant, will relate directly with gentiles. Jews and gentiles will actually be one now. The apostle Paul reassures new gentile believers in Ephesus about their inclusion in this new covenant:

> Therefore, remember that formerly you who are gentiles by birth and called "uncircumcised" by those who call themselves "the circumcision" (which is done in the body by human hands)—remember that at that time you were separate from Christ, excluded from citizenship in Israel and foreigners to the covenants of the promise, without hope and without God in the world. But now in Christ Jesus you who once were far away have been brought near by the blood of Christ.
>
> For he himself is our peace, who has made the two groups one and has destroyed the barrier, the dividing wall of hostility, by setting aside in his flesh the law with its commands and regulations. His purpose was to create in himself one new humanity out of the two, thus making peace, and in one body to reconcile both of them to God through the cross, by which he put to death their hostility. He came and preached peace to you who were far away and peace to those who were near. For through him we both have access to the Father by one Spirit.
>
> Consequently, you are no longer foreigners and strangers, but fellow citizens with God's people and also members of his household, built on the foundation of the apostles and prophets, with Christ Jesus himself as the chief cornerstone. In him the whole building is joined together and rises to become a holy temple in the Lord. And in him you too are being built together to become a dwelling in which God lives by his Spirit. (Eph 2:11–22)
>
> This mystery is that through the gospel the Gentiles are heirs together with Israel, members together of one body, and sharers together in the promise in Christ Jesus. (Eph 3:6)[18]

---

17. Those "under the law" refers to Jews and those "apart from the law" refers to gentiles.

18. Paul's reference to the "uncircumcision" and "circumcision" just means "gentile" and "Jew" said in another way. Male Israelites were circumcised on the eighth day after birth, and non-Jews were circumcised when they converted as a sign of being in the covenant. There was no physical initiation rite for women. The "mystery" in Ephesians 3:6 means that there is a previously hidden element to the new covenant, namely that the gentiles are now direct heirs to the promise of salvation through Jesus Christ.

Even though there were prophecies that hinted at the gentiles being included sometime in the future, it came as a shock to Jews of Jesus' day. There is a dramatic encounter between the apostle Peter, a God-fearing Roman centurion named Cornelius (a gentile), and two visions from God (Acts 10). God spoke to Cornelius in a dream that he needed to send for a man named Peter, who was then in the nearby city of Joppa, to come and speak to him. At the same time God gave Peter a vision of a tablecloth descending from heaven filled with all kinds of food, some of which was forbidden for a Jew to eat. This symbol was telling Peter that *all* people are now welcome directly into God's family. Being entreated to come, Peter traveled to Cornelius's house and found a large and receptive gathering. Cornelius retold his vision to Peter, and Peter then spoke the good news of Jesus' teachings, death and resurrection, and forgiveness of sins through him. All there were filled with the Holy Spirit and subsequently baptized, making this the first time the gospel had been preached to and responded to positively by gentiles. Later, God specifically called Paul to preach the gospel to the gentiles, which he did on several missionary journeys.

Essential Steps to Joining the New Covenant

Just as with the first covenant, which required sorrow for sin and a turning of the heart and will away from sin and toward loving God (repentance), the new covenant confirms that these elements are just as essential for a person to enter it. The first gospel message from the apostle Peter to hearers gathered for the Feast of Pentecost after Jesus' resurrection included this necessary charge. He told them God made this Jesus, whom they crucified, both Lord and Christ. With their conscience pricked they asked what they should do. Peter told them to repent of their sinful ways, be baptized, and they would receive the gift of the Holy Spirit (Acts 2).

Another necessary response is belief or faith. When the apostles preached they told their hearers to "believe the gospel" (Mark 1:15) and to "believe in Jesus" (John 3:16; 6:29; 20:31; Acts 16:31; Rom 10:9). These words come from NT Greek words, transliterated as *pisteuo* (a verb meaning to believe in something or someone, to rely on or trust with obedience the implied complement) and the related noun form, *pistis*. These words signify that to follow God is to believe that the message of the gospel is true, that you entrust your life to God the Father and his son Jesus, and that you intend to follow this up with obedience to God for as long as you live.[19] These concepts of repentance and faith/trust seem logical if a person

19. A story illustrates the nature of faith. There were a group of people surrounding

really desires to turn from their old selfish ways and turn toward loving God supremely. Remember that earlier we discussed the model of the big *S* (self) on the throne of a person's life, and becoming a Christian is taking ourselves off and putting God on that same throne. Any covenant with God by nature requires this sort of response.

Comparisons that Give Us a Deeper Understanding of the New Covenant

So far we have seen God's effort to deal with human sin and the estrangement it produces is best described as a reconciliation. "Reconciliation" is a relationship word. It is not just an analogy word—it is an accurate description of *what actually happens* when that relationship is restored. We give up our old selfish ways and humbly bow before God, realizing we have created a great rift between ourselves and him, and that we have no power within us to undo our wrongs or mend ourselves. We realize the depth of our sin and turn toward God, entrusting our whole future into his hands. But this by no means cancels our sins or restores the relationship. The death and resurrection of Jesus shows God has overcome the obstacles that kept us apart. Jesus is the ultimate priest *and* priestly sacrifice that atones for our sins; he willingly became our substitute. God had no obligation to do this for us; it is a gift of grace that goes far beyond what we deserve. His grace went so far as to give his followers the Holy Spirit to live inside them and include the gentiles as direct heirs of the covenant. So in our context, "reconciliation" is a grace-filled word that describes the great lengths God went to to bring us back to himself.

But there are other comparisons and word-pictures that give us a richer appreciation of the kind of blessing being reconciled to God is.

Sacrifice

We have already talked about the idea of Jesus being the final sacrifice for the sins of humanity—a substitute of the sufferings and death of Jesus for

---

a daredevil who said he could cross the river gorge in front of them on a tightrope with a grooved-wheel wheelbarrow. They had seen him warming up and could see he had very good balancing skills. When he asked them if they believed he could cross the whole gorge with his wheelbarrow many of them said, "Yes, I bet you can." The daredevil responded, "Well, who wants to be the first in the wheelbarrow?" No one took him up on his offer. Real belief, real faith, real trust, gets in God's wheelbarrow and lets God take us where he wills.

the suffering and death we earned by sinning. This means God was taking the initiative to self-sacrifice himself on our behalf, a very humbling action. Consider Paul's words to the Philippians about Christ's attitude when he came to save us:

> *Who, being in very nature God, did not consider equality with God something to be used to his own advantage; rather, he made himself nothing by taking the very nature of a servant, being made in human likeness. And being found in appearance as a man,*
>   *he humbled himself by becoming obedient to death—even death on a cross! Therefore God exalted him to the highest place and gave him the name that is above every name,*
>   *that at the name of Jesus every knee should bow, in heaven and on earth and under the earth, and every tongue acknowledge that Jesus Christ is Lord, to the glory of God the Father.* (Phil 2:6–11)

The first step came from the one offended—God! The idea of sacrifice is further illustrated when the apostle John described Jesus as "the Lamb of God, who takes away the sin of the world" (John 1:29, 36; Rev 5:6). He is the sacrificial Lamb, just as the lamb was sacrificed in the OT to atone for sins.

Redemption

Redemption is a very prominent metaphor for what Jesus did for us. To redeem has to do with releasing from bondage, to set free, to emancipate, or to purchase the same. Redemption occurred when slaves were bought from the slaveholder and then set free. They were once in bondage but now have been set free by some benevolent person. The concept of "ransom" is included here where something valuable is exchanged for the release of a captive. But what are we freed from?

> Christ redeems his followers from sin, the condemnation of the law and death. According to the NT, "Everyone who commits sin is a slave to sin" (John 8:34). Sinners are "slaves to sin, which leads to death" (Rom 6:16). This is the spiritual bondage from which sinners need to be redeemed, and the language of that redemption retains the OT connotations of a price that has been paid to secure the freedom of slaves. We thus read that "redemption . . . came by Christ Jesus" (Rom 3:24), who "redeemed us from the curse of the law by becoming a curse for us" (Gal 3:13). Christ came "to redeem those under law" (Gal 4:5) and "gave himself for us to redeem us from all wickedness" (Titus 2:14). One of the most vivid pictures is this one: God "has

rescued us from the dominion of darkness and brought us into the kingdom of the Son he loves, in whom we have redemption, the forgiveness of sins" (Col 1:13–14).[20]

So the freedom Christ brings is the freedom of forgiveness, freedom from the curse of the law, which was death, and freedom from slavery to sin—we don't have to do it anymore! But what are we freed *to*? The other side of redemption is that we now have a new and loving master—God himself. We are not our own (1 Cor 6:19–20); we have become new slaves to righteousness and holiness (Rom 6:18, 19). But there is still more to come—the final redemption will occur when God will redeem even our bodies (heaven and the new heavens and earth—discussed in the next chapter) and the whole physical creation itself will be freed from its decay (Rom 8:18–25). God is making and will continue to make all things new.

Salvation

The word "salvation" is used often to describe what happens when someone believes, and God the Father and Jesus are frequently referred to as Savior. Like redemption, to be saved is to be saved from some peril and rescued to a much better condition of health and safety. "By far the most common NT use of salvation . . . has to do with salvation from sin ('and you shall call his name Jesus, for he will save his people from their sins,' Matt 1:21 RSV). To be precise, one is saved from the *penalty* of sin (Luke 7:48, 50), from the *power* of sin (Rom 6:12–14) and from the *practice* of sin as a way of life (1 John 3:9–10; 5:18)."[21]

What does it feel like to be saved? Almost universally the response is gratitude and a desire to respond in love. And, if the peril was our own fault, we vow to not do it again—we'll pay very close attention next time. Here is a story of being saved from a physical danger in which the danger was hidden (see footnote).[22] It illustrates what is also true in the spiritual life—we often don't sense our spiritual danger because of ignorance or just neglect.

Victory

Victory is a persuasive goal for many in today's world. Athletes are spurred on to victory on the field to win a medal, a trophy, or money to show they

---

20. Ryken et al., "Redemption," 699.
21. Ryken et al., "Salvation," 753.
22. Jabakhanji, "London Man Saves Family."

have conquered all other competitors. Financial victory is having adequate money to meet all our needs (and frequently our wants). Victory at the polls means one candidate has more votes than any other. Personal victories can be overcoming a bad habit or achieving a goal we've worked long and hard for.

The battleground for our souls is a contest that God can help anyone be victorious in. This battleground is between the person and the enemies of their own desires, sinful influences, and the devil. This victory began when Jesus confronted Satan or other demons who had possessed people. He frequently spoke to them and cast them out (Mark 5:1–20) and even gave his disciples the ability to do the same (Luke 10:17–20; Acts 16:16–18).

The victory is over more than just satanic powers. Paul asked the Roman Christians:

> *Who shall separate us from the love of Christ? Shall trouble or hardship or persecution or famine or nakedness or danger or sword? . . . No, in all these things we are more than conquerors through him who loved us. For I am convinced that neither death nor life, neither angels nor demons, neither the present nor the future, nor any powers, neither height nor depth, nor anything else in all creation, will be able to separate us from the love of God that is in Christ Jesus our Lord.* (Rom 8:35, 37–39)

So, there is nothing on this earth that can separate us from God. He is victorious over all "foreign" powers that might seek to defeat us—powers such as governments, oppressive laws, cultural norms and morality, tradition, and powerful individuals. There is victory over internal enemies as well—our own sinful desires, personality tendencies, and anything else that would push us toward sin (Rom 6; 8). Jesus' earthly ministry also demonstrated his power over physical illness. When he went preaching the gospel he frequently healed the sicknesses and diseases of his hearers (Matt 4:23; 9:35). He even gave his disciples the ability to heal and cast out demons in his name (Matt 10:8; Acts 3:1–10; Acts 5:12–16). Still today there are occasions where evil spirits need to be exorcised and physical bodies need healing. God works healing miracles today, but he is in charge of when he acts. God wants us to pray for each other in faith so that healings and reconciliations occur (Jas 5:13–20). We need to leave the results in his hands—we ask and he answers in his wisdom.

God helps us to be victorious in all these areas, but as discussed earlier, we must also participate with attitudes and acts of trust and commitment. The final victory over all our spiritual and physical foes waits for what happens after death.

Justification/Being Made Right

If we've ever been the subject of a criminal trial, we know the exhilaration of a "not guilty" verdict. We also know the relief when a wrong we've done to someone else is made right—there is confession and forgiveness and a sense of freedom and restoration comes over us. "Justification" is a word that comes from the legal world and has a lot of relational context, since there are at least two parties/persons involved. When someone is justified, he/she is made right with the other person—whatever differences there were have been settled. The apostle Paul talks a lot about these ideas in his letter to the Romans, who included both Jews and gentiles. The Jews thought they could be made right with God by obeying all the laws of the Mosaic covenant. Paul reminds them that they have all sinned so the law can not justify or make them right with God anymore, and since gentiles have all sinned as well, they are likewise in the same boat. He reminds them that their ancestor, Abraham, was justified before God because he believed in what God said, trusted him, and obeyed his commands. Like Abraham, Paul's readers had to do the same if they ever hoped to be right with God.[23] We can experience that same "rightness" when we act toward God like Abraham did and feel the freedom and peace he did.

Eternal Life

When you read the gospel of John you often see the words "eternal life" used by Jesus. We humans know what it is like to be "alive," and we also have a concept of death. We often think of death as ceasing to be, to have no more consciousness. Eternal life seems so appealing because we all know we are going to die physically and some of us are not sure what is on the other side, if anything. It can lead to a great deal of fear. We've also already talked about both physical and spiritual death, both of them ultimately a result of sin. Much of Christ's victory in the atonement is over sin and death. Paul describes death as "the last enemy" (1 Cor 15:26). He also says it can be defeated:

---

23. There is debate among Christians about the meaning of Paul's use of the word "faith" in reference to being justified. For instance, in Galatians 2:20 Paul says, "I have been crucified with Christ and I no longer live, but Christ lives in me. The life I now live in the body, I live by faith in the Son of God, who loved me and gave himself for me." The NIV Bible translators say "faith *in* the Son of God," but other scholars make a good case that it can just as easily mean "the *faithfulness of* the Son of God." However, both these concepts are true. If we ever hope to be made right with God then we must live out faith/trust in God's faithfulness.

> *When the perishable has been clothed with the imperishable, and the mortal with immortality, then the saying that is written will come true: "Death has been swallowed up in victory."*
> *"Where, O death, is your victory?*
> *Where, O death, is your sting?"*
> *The sting of death is sin, and the power of sin is the law. But thanks be to God! He gives us the victory through our Lord Jesus Christ.* (1 Cor 15:54–57)

Much of the spoils of victory (eternal life) are implied to be after physical death, in heaven or the new heavens and earth. John, near the end of the book of Revelation, says, "He will wipe every tear from their eyes. There will be no more death or mourning or crying or pain, for the old order of things has passed away" (Rev 21:4). But it will be more than the lack of earthly sorrows. It will be a never-ending and living relationship with Jesus, his Father, and the Holy Spirit (Remember the Trinity?). Bible references suggest this vibrant life will be beyond anything we can imagine. Paul says, "For now we see only a reflection as in a mirror; then we shall see face to face. Now I know in part; then I shall know fully, even as I am fully known" (1 Cor 13:12).

But the eternal life God brings doesn't *start* after death, *it begins now*! He said to fellow Jew Nicodemus, who was beginning to follow him, "Very truly I tell you, no one can see the kingdom of God unless they are born again" (John 3:3). He said to Jewish leaders, "Very truly I tell you, whoever hears my word and believes him who sent me has eternal life and will not be judged but has crossed over from death to life" (John 5:24). Later, he compares himself to a good shepherd who lays his life down to protect his sheep from thieves or wolves. He says of his sheep, "I have come that they may have life, and have it to the full" (John 10:10b). Paul echoes the same idea, "Therefore, if anyone is in Christ, the new creation has come. The old has gone, the new is here" (2 Cor 5:17)!

Sometimes it is hard for us to appreciate this great thing God has done—to abolish death and give us new life. This appreciation seems to be felt very keenly by those who have survived a brush with death. Besides being thankful, they often feel a renewed appreciation for every new day. They try to live life with more intentionality and for a worthy purpose. They stop and smell the roses more. I think of the WWII movie *Saving Private Ryan*, in which Captain John Miller (played by Tom Hanks) leads an elite quad of Army Rangers to save a young soldier, James Ryan (played by Matt Damon), from the intense fighting behind enemy lines because Ryan's three brothers have already been killed in combat. General George Marshall is determined to save Ryan's mother from a fourth telegram of condolence by sending eight men into harm's way to save one. At the end of the movie the squad has been successful in finding him, but Captain Miller lies dying in the wake. Ryan comes up to Miller, who looks intently into Ryan's eyes, and tells the young soldier, "Earn this." In other words, don't waste your life. Live a life worthy of the sacrifice we've just made for you. Next we flash forward and we see Ryan coming back to Normandy many years later to visit the grave of Captain John Miller. He is now an old man, and with his family in tow he looks intensely at the marble cross and asks himself, "Did I earn it? Did I live a good life? Was my subsequent life a fitting response to the sacrifice made for me?" Likewise, Jesus asks the same type of question of us, "Are you living in a way that honors the sacrifice I made for you, my life for yours, to save you from the *eternal* peril of your own selfishness? Have you started experiencing eternal life *now*?"

Baptism

Baptism is very much related to the idea of eternal life. Much like circumcision was a marker of having entered the old covenant, so in the NT baptism signifies we have entered the new covenant. The NT records that everyone who repented of sin and trusted Jesus Christ as Savior was commanded to be and was soon after baptized (Matt 28:19; Acts 2:36–41). Baptism was a physical representation of what had just happened spiritually—as the person went under the water this signified being buried with Christ and the old way of life was now dead. As he or she was raised up out of the water this signified that new life had come, that person had now been raised from the dead, just like Christ, and now had new life in him (Rom 6:3–4; Col 2:11–12).

Adoption/Children/Marriage

The family is a powerful metaphor for the reconciliation God brings to us. Many of our dearest and most lasting relationships come from there. The adoption metaphor is especially meaningful for gentiles, who were "grafted into" God's family in a direct way in the new covenant (Rom 11). The adoption concept comes from Paul, who uses it five times in his writings. This is a small number, but it fits very well with the existing truth that those who follow God are his "children." This idea is prominent in both the OT and NT. Further, in the NT letters the recipients are frequently addressed as "children," "brothers," and "sisters," again highlighting the idea that God's people are a family. Jesus said whoever did his Father's will is his brother, sister, or mother (Mark 3:33–34). The idea of children is of course not biological but spiritual and relational. Many times in the OT God chastised Israel for being children of idols rather than children of his (Jer 2:26–28; Mal 2:11–12). The apostle John warned Christians that if they want to hold the name of "children of God," then they should act like it by continuing to do what is right and to love one another (1 John 3:10).

The idea of children also implies the idea of subordination. We are not in charge, God is. He is the leader, the head, the Father, and we are children. We are immature but seeking maturity; we lack knowledge and seek hard for wisdom. We need a divine Father in every way in our spiritual life just like a child needs a loving parent.

The idea of subordination is also seen in the marriage metaphor. Paul reminds the Ephesian church that Christ is their head like the husband is the head of the wife, and he loves the church (his children) like a husband loves his wife (Eph 5:22–33). Christ went so far as to sacrifice himself for the church to make her holy and blameless, just like a husband should do all he can to help his wife be pure and holy. In response the church should submit to Christ as a wife submits to a loving husband. Paul even uses a more intimate metaphor, suggesting when a husband and wife are physically intimate that this helps explain the mystery of Christ and the church. Similarly, Christ is called the "bridegroom" and the church his "bride" (John 3:29; Rev 19:7). This intimate portrait hints at the greater closeness that God's people will have with him in heaven when our earth-bound barriers are removed. Then we will see him as Paul said earlier, "face to face" (1 Cor 13:12).

To close this section, I recommend reading the article cited in the footnote. It's a story of adoption between an eight-year-old boy and a single man. It highlights the feelings that God has toward his children and hopefully how God's children look at him.[24] Make sure you read it!

A Kingdom

Most of us have read our share of children's stories of kingdoms with their kings, queens, princes and princesses, knights and maidens, fair lands, ships, tradesmen and -women, peasants, and everything else that goes with those stories. We understand there is leadership there, sometimes good and sometimes bad, people that are ruled, relationships with neighboring kingdoms, and some vast area of land that makes up the realm. The biblical story has many of these same elements. In the beginning there was Eden with God the benevolent King, animals, plants, water creatures, a fertile

24 San Filippo, "I've Wanted to Be Adopted."

garden, and Adam and Eve as hopefully benevolent stewards of it all. There is Israel, God's chosen people. Again, God was their king, and it included a land, its resources, neighbors, laws and statues to govern by, and human leaders who would hopefully rule under God and be a light on a hill to those around it. You were born into this kingdom if you were an Israelite, but foreigners could also join it. The kingdom prospered or declined based on the stewardship, conduct, and character of the leaders and people. God was the head, but he did not rule by force unless absolutely necessary. It was to be a kingdom based on love, faithfulness, goodness, and obedience.

Likewise, the definition of the kingdom of God in the NT is about a place but seems to be more about God and his people who are in it. The kingdom has been defined as God's rule over his people and the whole created order. Jesus talked a lot about this and his parables and stories illustrated what it is like. Many of them show how valuable it is to those who are in it and how it grows, like the parable of scattering seeds, a hidden treasure, a pearl of great price, a fishing dragnet, yeast hidden in bread, an unforgiving debtor, the workers paid equally, the wedding feast, and a mustard seed. It is worth reading all of these. Jesus taught his disciples to want to be in it (Matt 6:33), that it could be inside them (Luke 17:21), and this was like being born a second time (John 3:3). Jesus describes what those in it acted like and valued—humility, righteousness, mercy, purity of heart, peace, and the willingness to suffer for righteousness (see the Beatitudes in Matt 5:1–20, Matt 18:1–4). Certain people disqualify themselves from being in it by their evil conduct (1 Cor 6:9–10). When his kingdom was near, miracles happened (Matt 12:22–28; Luke 10:9). It is not only present now, but will come in fullness later (Matt 16:27–28, Christ's second coming). It will never end (Luke 1:33).

So, when a person becomes a Christian she becomes part of a kingdom with the most benevolent and powerful king possible. There is protection and the companionship of fellow members. We are not alone. We are part of something bigger than ourselves and very good. We can relax. We belong.

Other Metaphors

There are other biblical metaphors that describe what it means to be a Christian:

- God is a caring shepherd and we are sheep.
- Lost and now found.
- Dirty and now clean.

- Broken but now mended.
- Sick but now made well or healed.

They suggest something bad is now good or something dangerous is now safe. They all either give one true aspect of what it means to come to know God or are a good analogy of it. There is nothing else like it in human experience, and it takes many ways of looking at it to give us the fullest picture of what knowing God is like.

Growth toward Maturity

This reconciliation with all the words we've used above is designed to be constantly deepening. After a person initially comes to know God, then that relationship is meant to deepen over a lifetime. This is because God's goal is both to forgive *and* transform—to make us more like he is. He wants us to grow up spiritually and live out the two Great Commandments of love to him and others, empowered by the Holy Spirit. Christ especially wanted his followers to love *each other* sacrificially. He said to the first disciples, "A new command I give you: Love one another. As I have loved you, so you must love one another. By this everyone will know that you are my disciples, if you love one another" (John 13:34–35). Paul also reminded his Galatian readers of these very things—to do good to all people, especially those in the family of faith (Gal 6:10). We can only do this supernatural "loving" as we walk in step with God's Spirit:

> *So I say, walk by the Spirit, and you will not gratify the desires of the flesh . . . The acts of the flesh are obvious: sexual immorality, impurity and debauchery; idolatry and witchcraft; hatred, discord, jealousy, fits of rage, selfish ambition, dissensions, factions and envy; drunkenness, orgies, and the like. I warn you, as I did before, that those who live like this will not inherit the kingdom of God.*
>
> *But the fruit of the Spirit is love, joy, peace, forbearance, kindness, goodness, faithfulness, gentleness and self-control. Against such things there is no law. Those who belong to Christ Jesus have crucified the flesh with its passions and desires. Since we live by the Spirit, let us keep in step with the Spirit.* (Gal 5:16, 19–25)

This process of gradually becoming more Christlike is described with a variety of words in the NT. We see words like sanctification, transformed, becoming Christlike, being holy, being righteous, becoming mature or complete/perfect, to be clean or pure in heart. Sometimes non-Christians critique Christians for not being immediately and completely holy as Jesus is. This is an unrealistic expectation and can even be a hidden one in the heart of a new Christian. She expects her character to be quickly transformed in a matter of months to that of Jesus'. This can lead to unnecessary heartache and discouragement. This is not an excuse, however, for we are never to excuse sin but instead to confess and repent of the sins we commit—both to God and to those we have wronged. There is a bumper stick that speaks to this issue. It says, "Please be patient. God isn't finished with me yet." There is truth in this, but again, it can not be used as an excuse for ungodly behavior or attitudes.

God is patient, but his goals are high for us. C. S. Lewis illustrates this growth process and what the Christian is in for. He says of God, who will,

> in the long run, be satisfied with nothing less than absolute perfection, will also be delighted with the first feeble, stumbling effort you make tomorrow to do the simplest duty. As a great Christian writer (George MacDonald) pointed out, every father is pleased at the baby's first attempt to walk: no father would be satisfied with anything less than a firm, free, manly walk in a grown-up son. In the same way, he said, 'God is easy to please but hard to satisfy' . . .
>
> Here is another way of putting the two sides of the truth. On the one hand we must never imagine that our own unaided efforts can be relied on to carry us even through the next twenty-four hours as "decent" people. If He does not support us, not one of us is safe from some gross sin. On the other hand, no possible degree of holiness or heroism which has ever been recorded of the greatest saints is beyond what he is determined to produce in every one of us in the end . . .
>
> That is why we must not be surprised if we are in for a rough time . . . God is forcing him [us] on, or up, to a higher level: putting him into situations where he will have to be very much braver, or more patient, or more loving, than he ever dreamed of being before . . .
>
> Imagine yourself as a living house. God comes in to rebuild that house. At first, perhaps, you can understand what He is doing . . . But presently he starts knocking the house about in a way that hurts abominably and does not seem to make sense . . . The explanation is that He is building quite a different house from the one you thought of—You thought you were going to be made into a decent little cottage: but He is building a palace. He intends to come and live in it Himself.[25]

---

25. Lewis, *Mere Christianity*, 174–76.

Living and Spreading Reconciliation: The Church

Christian maturing was never intended to happen through a "Lone Ranger" experience but to happen in community. There is strength in living life together. This means no Christian should feel she is on her own and that success in pleasing God is due to her own efforts alone. The church is Christ's body, spiritually and physically, on earth. He is gone physically, but he left a multitude of disciples in his stead. Using an orchestra analogy, each one has a part to play and each has to play her part in harmony with the others. Then there will be beautiful, melodious music. This is why, before Christ was crucified and exalted to heaven, he prayed that his church would be unified, that it would truly show what he was like, and so that many would believe in him because of their life and testimony (John 17). They were to be a light on a hill—together—just like Israel was supposed to be.

We've already stated that Christ's disciples are to love *each other*. How is that shown? We are to help each other overcome sin (Gal 6:1; Jas 5:19–29), carry each other's burdens (Gal 6:2), be kind and compassionate toward one another (Eph 4:32), forgive each other (Eph 4:32), encourage each other (Heb 10:25), sing together (Col 3:16), humbly serve each other as Christ served us (Phil 2:1–11), and honor each other (Rom 12:10). Each member depends on the other, and even the most humble servant is of great value. When one suffers, so do the rest. When one is honored, all share in it (1 Cor 12:12–26). God designed the Christian life to be lived in community, and it is there that the Christian finds his greatest help and the vehicle through which he can be of greatest service.

Reconciliation Broadcast

If reconciliation is the best thing that could ever happen to a person, and it is, then the most natural thing is to want others to experience it. Part of the nature of love is sharing it. Sharing God's love naturally includes loving the world (all people) and doing our best to bring those in our sphere of influence into a relationship with him. Some of Jesus' last words are in this regard. He has been raised from the dead and is about to ascend into heaven. He tells his disciples:

> *All authority in heaven and on earth has been given to me. Therefore go and make disciples of all nations, baptizing them in the name of the Father and of the Son and of the Holy Spirit, and teaching them to obey everything I have commanded you. And surely I am with you always, to the very end of the age.* (Matt 28:18–20)

Soon after this he sends the Holy Spirit down on the day of Pentecost to fill and empower his disciples for this very task (Acts 1). Much of Christian history describes this process of broadcasting. Jesus sent his disciples out to testify about him. The apostle Paul was sent by God to preach the gospel to Jews and especially to gentiles. He went on three missionary journeys into what is now Europe to spread God's message of reconciliation and to establish healthy churches. This process of trying to bring others into the faith is frequently called "evangelism" and "discipleship." This desire to see others come to know God has been a major heartbeat of the church up to this day. Many churches spend a significant chunk of their budget on missions and encourage the sending of members to be missionaries.

But why hasn't God just done this himself? He would surely do it best. Why couldn't Jesus just be perpetually "here" on earth? I don't know. That would have been my plan. Contrary to our logic, God seems to have delegated a good share of what he wants to now accomplish in this world to his sometimes inadequate church. For himself, it is difficult to say when God acts directly in this world because he doesn't announce it! But he surely has given his church a charge to spread reconciliation and to do good to all. So let's look at the church's record—how well has Jesus' admonition to his first followers (and current believers) to love each other, to love the world, and to spread his gospel been fulfilled? Sometimes well and other times poorly. The history of the church is such that we can find many examples of great love, goodness, courage, generosity, and sacrifice, and at other times we can see strife, greed, pride, and indifference.[26] The church is an imperfect witness, but it is still God's chosen vessel to encourage and mature his family and to show his love to the world. Can anyone say, then, at the end of their life as they stand before God's judgment seat, that it is the church's fault they did not respond positively to the gospel? No, God loves each one of us and wants each person to know him—that's why he made us! He gives each one opportunities and he surely speaks directly to our hearts (see the story of my Muslim friend from the Congo later in this chapter). No one is going to get a raw deal from God.

---

26. See Schmidt, *How Christianity*; and Dickson, *Bullies and Saints*, for how the church brought much good and some strife to this world. Individual readers will likely have both good and bad stories that relate to the church's behavior and to possibly their own encounters with Christians.

How Heavenly Is the Reconciled Life?

Much of our reaction to the events of our life is colored by our expectations. Positive expectations are frequently healthy and can give us a positive outlook on life. Negative expectations can sometimes lead to an overly pessimistic view of our destiny. The trick is to be positive about the things we can change for the good, with God as our motivator and empowerer. Further, when we trust in the promises found in the Bible, we can be sure God will be faithful to come through. Christians should channel their expectations according to God's promises and the experience of other believers throughout history. The experience of past believers plus our own shows us that life in this world is difficult, for the Christian or anyone else. The question is whether we have given a heavenly Father permission to filter everything that comes our way. A famous quotation of the apostle Paul is, "And we know that in all things God works for the good of those who love him, who have been called according to his purpose" (Rom 8:28). For the Christian good can be brought out of any evil done to us. This does not mean that everything that happens to a Christian is good, but God can bring some sort of redemption out of it. We can think back on the Roman persecutions of Christians in the first centuries. This was certainly not "good," but God used it to test and mature his children and to be a testimony to the world of the disciples' love for them. Some suffered physical torture and death and were promoted to the blessings of heaven. In the current day Christians in the West seldom suffer greatly for their faith, but there is great evidence of persecution in certain Asian and African countries.[27] The future is no brighter. The apostle John records the revelation of Jesus regarding the suffering of Christians in the future at the hands of ungodly rulers (Rev 11–13). The Christian must take the long view of all this, remembering what awaits. Paul reminded fellow believers, "I consider that our present sufferings are not worth comparing with the glory that will be revealed in us" (Rom 8:18).

So, how should a Christian view this life? Can she expect any more earthly "comfort" than anyone else? From God? A big yes. From the church? Usually. From those outside the church or those antagonistic to its mission? Likely not, and sometimes strong resistance. From Satan and his demons? A big no—expect antagonism. Paul and Barnabas concluded, "We must go through many hardships to enter the kingdom of God" (Acts 14:22b). As we noted in chapter 1, God frequently uses trials and sufferings to both test and mature his children. We noted that there is also the real spiritual battle that Satan brings to Christians. Sometimes Christians fail to realize they are in a

---

27. See Open Doors, "Christian Persecution"; or Voice of the Martyrs, "Home," for evidence of present-day persecution.

spiritual battle here on earth and that they have an enemy that pursues them subtly. He wants them to fail, and uses his influences to push them to think and act wrongly. He tempts where he thinks they are weak, tries to get them to believe lies about God and other believers, discourages good prayer and devotional habits that keep them close to God, and any other strategy that will thwart God's plans for them.[28] They may also not be aware that God is more powerful than any temptation and any tempter and that he will always give enough strength to stand against anything evil. And if evil comes our way, God can use it for good (Rom 8:28). God is trying to make each of us beautiful. It is like refining gold—we need our impurities burned off. God is very resourceful—he will cause Satan's efforts to backfire—to use the trials that come from evil done against us to make us better followers of him. We must remember that trials (and sometimes persecutions) are no more than Jesus ever promised. He clearly said that his early followers would be persecuted like he was (John 15:20). The apostle Peter reminded his fellow believers:

> *Dear friends, do not be surprised at the fiery ordeal that has come on you to test you, as though something strange were happening to you. But rejoice inasmuch as you participate in the sufferings of Christ, so that you may be overjoyed when his glory is revealed. If you are insulted because of the name of Christ, you are blessed, for the Spirit of glory and of God rests on you. If you suffer, it should not be as a murderer or thief or any other kind of criminal, or even as a meddler. However, if you suffer as a Christian, do not be ashamed, but praise God that you bear that name. For it is time for judgment to begin with God's household; and if it begins with us, what will the outcome be for those who do not obey the gospel of God? And,*
>   *"If it is hard for the righteous to be saved,*
>   *what will become of the ungodly and the sinner?"*
> *So then, those who suffer according to God's will should commit themselves to their faithful Creator and continue to do good.*
> (1 Pet 4:12–19)

How spiritually satisfying our Christian life is can also vary according to our own personality and emotional tendencies. I've found comfort in reading books like Brant Hansen's *Blessed are the Misfits*. I share some of his struggles, as do many others—just read the appendix of his book! Brant has

---

28. We noted a book earlier, *The Screwtape Letters* by C. S. Lewis, which describes a fictional but realistic account of how demons might work to undermine a person's relationship with God. This is a good source for how Satan might work for ill in a Christian's life.

Asperger's syndrome and does not react emotionally like most people and has difficulty in social interactions. This has affected his emotional reactions to God and others, his ability to pray, and his struggles with the expectations of extrovert-dominated church leaders. The subtitle is *Great News for Believers Who Are Introverts, Spiritual Strugglers, or Just Feel Like They're Missing Something.* Sometimes in Christianity there is a tendency for leaders to suggest that the Christian life is one blessing after another, filled with constant victory over sin, dominated by a perpetual positive attitude and a feeling of God's presence. For many this is not the case, and it is not because of anything sinful. One has only to look at the recently discovered writings of Mother Theresa, one of the most respected Christians of this last century. Her life was dedicated to service to the poor and to spreading the love of Jesus. Her private writings, revealed in the book *Mother Theresa, Come Be My Light* by Brian Kolodiejchuk, describe an inner spiritual life that was frequently devoid of the emotional satisfaction one might expect for one so holy. There were long seasons where she did not feel God's presence and felt alone. It was like trying to see God in the dark. But she knew God was there and she loved him and was faithful to him regardless of her feelings.

There are no doubt Christians who have a very satisfying emotional experience when they pray, sing, read the Scriptures, fellowship, or hear spirited sermons. Their experience is a blessing and should be cherished. Church history has examples of mystics who had wonderful emotional relationships with God. Most of the rest of God's people likely have some experience in between. This variety reminds us that we are all individuals and our relationship to God is not based on feelings but on his promises and knowing his love toward us. We can know God is smiling on us when we do as he has asked us. Loving and being loved is not necessarily a special way of feeling!

Life Is to Be Enjoyed

Though life on this planet is sometimes difficult, God intended it to be enjoyed. Even when we daily see the effects of sin around us, God asks us to focus on our relationship with him as our true source of joy, peace, and comfort. He has also given us things in this life that are meant to be enjoyed (1 Tim 6:17). Some swing to the far sides of the pendulum in this area—some engage in extreme asceticism and some in extreme hedonism—both of which are harmful. Randy Alcorn gives us some good guidance:

> God isn't displeased when we enjoy a good meal, marital sex, a football game, a cozy fire, or a good book. He's not up in Heaven

frowning at us and saying, "Stop it—you should only find joy in me." This would be as foreign to God's nature as our heavenly Father as it would be to mine as an earthly father if I gave my daughters a Christmas gift and started pouting because they enjoyed it too much. No, I gave the gift to bring joy to them and to me—if they didn't take pleasure in it, I'd be disappointed. Their pleasure in my gift to them draws them closer to me. I am *delighted* that they enjoy the gift.

Of course, if children become so preoccupied with the gift that they walk away from their father and ignore him, that's different. Though preoccupation with a God-given gift can turn to idolatry, enjoying that same gift with a grateful heart can draw us closer to God.

All secondary joys are *derivative* in nature. They cannot be separated from God. Flowers are beautiful for one reason—God is beautiful. Rainbows are stunning because God is stunning. Puppies are delightful because God is delightful. Sports are fun because God is fun. Study is rewarding because God is rewarding. Work is fulfilling because God is fulfilling.[29]

So the Christian should feel happy about enjoying God's gifts. When he was done with creation God called it all "very good." He is the author of all that is good and wants his children to enjoy the earthly blessings he has provided.

How Hellish Is the Unreconciled Life?

We've talked a lot about being reconciled to God. The unreconciled life, as we saw in chapter 2, will have trouble in this life and the next. We were designed to love and serve God and when we don't do that our lives do not go well, even if they appear to on the surface. We've talked about the earthly consequences of sin, but the consequences for those who reject God's overtures of reconciliation continue after death. Hell awaits those who refuse to serve God. Hell is a place, whether spiritual or spiritual/physical is hard to say, but it is definitely a place of suffering and torment. There will be "darkness, where there will be weeping and gnashing of teeth" (think of aloneness, great sorrow, and extreme regret, Matt 8:12). People will be tormented by what they have done in this life (Luke 16:23), surrounded by unquenchable fire (Luke 16:24; Matt 13:50). Worms will forever devour things (Mark 8:48). It is a punishment from God, and it lasts forever: "He

---

29. Alcorn, *Heaven*, 177.

will punish those who do not know God and do not obey the gospel of our Lord Jesus. They will be punished with everlasting destruction and shut out from the presence of the Lord and from the glory of his might . . ." (2 Thess 1:8–9; see also Matt 25:46). These verses give a hint at why hell is so "hellish." God did not have to make hell unpleasant with any angry intent on his part. Though he is angry with sinners, and hell is surely a punishment, hell is mostly hellish for the simple fact that *God is not there*. Whatever was good or loving is forever gone. Satan, demons, and all those opposed to God can now live like they wanted to live on earth—without God. But now they have more knowledge of who God is and who they are—what they neglected on earth they are now forced to know. Think of Jacob Marley. No wonder there is torment, the gnashing of teeth, darkness, and regret. Some speculate hell is hellish because each person will be alone, with an eternity to contemplate his or her fate. Regardless of the setting, the God of all love is now permanently gone from their presence.

What about Those Who Never Hear the Gospel?

A frequent question when one thinks about the consequences of our choices is about what happens to people, through no fault of their own, who have never heard about the God of the Bible, Jesus, or the good news of salvation through him. They never could choose God as he is revealed in the Bible. There are those who lived before the time of Jesus and who never heard about the nation of Israel and their mission to be a light for God to the nations. Some Christians relegate these people to hell. They claim salvation is for those who loved God supremely and their neighbors as themselves in the OT or those who hear the NT gospel and then repent and respond in faith toward God (certainly true but incomplete; Luke 10:25–37; John 1:12; 2 Thess 1:8–9). However, there is good evidence that God accepts all those who positively respond to whatever spiritual light (knowledge) they have. Paul reminded the Romans (especially the Jews) that those who sinned without any knowledge of the OT law (gentiles) will be judged by their own consciences:

> *For it is not those who hear the law who are righteous in God's sight, but it is those who obey the law who will be declared righteous. (Indeed, when Gentiles, who do not have the law, do by nature things required by the law, they are a law for themselves, even though they do not have the law. They show that the requirements of the law are written on their hearts, their consciences also bearing witness, and their thoughts sometimes accusing them and*

> at other times even defending them.) This will take place on the day when God judges people's secrets through Jesus Christ, as my gospel declares. (Rom 2:13–16)

It would seem grossly unfair if God did anything other than give these people a chance to respond to him. This is likely the reason we all have a conscience—he wants us all to have a reasonable chance to know and love him. That all will have a chance to know God is testified by the fact that one of his great characteristics is impartiality; he shows no favoritism (Rom 2:11).[30]

This idea is further confirmed when Paul reasoned with scholars at the Areopagus[31] in Athens. Athens, and Greece in general, had temples to worship many different gods, and, as Paul noticed, some in Athens had even erected an altar with the inscription, "To an Unknown God." These men were ignorant of many of the facts about Israel and Jesus, so he took the time to inform them:

> *The God who made the world and everything in it is the Lord of heaven and earth and does not live in temples built by human hands. And he is not served by human hands, as if he needed anything. Rather, he himself gives everyone life and breath and everything else. From one man he made all the nations, that they should inhabit the whole earth; and he marked out their appointed times in history and the boundaries of their lands. God did this so that they would seek him and perhaps reach out for him and find him, though he is not far from any one of us. "For in him we live and move and have our being." As some of your own poets have said, "We are his offspring." (Acts 17:24–28)*

The words "seek him and perhaps reach out for him" have also been translated as "feel their way toward him" or "grope for him." This gives the picture of someone feeling for something they can't see very clearly. They are seeking for God with the little spiritual light they have. Paul concludes that, even in this situation, God is not far from any one of us. Jesus earlier testified:

> *Ask and it will be given to you; seek and you will find; knock and the door will be opened to you. For everyone who asks receives; the one who seeks finds; and to the one who knocks, the door will be opened.*
>
> *Which of you, if your son asks for bread, will give him a stone? Or if he asks for a fish, will give him a snake? If you, then,*

---

30. There are others who think we will be given a chance after death to respond to the gospel. This is an interesting thought, but there is little biblical evidence it is true.

31. The Areopagus was a hill outside Athens covered in stone seats. It was used as a forum for the rulers of Athens to hold trials, debate, and discuss important matters.

> *though you are evil, know how to give good gifts to your children, how much more will your Father in heaven give good gifts to those who ask him!* (Matt 7:7–11)

God wants us to find him, even if our knowledge of him is limited. I relate a true story of a friend I met in our church in Denver who was born and grew up in the Democratic Republic of the Congo. There was (and is) much infighting in that nation among various factions with much bloodshed, even among the innocent. Attackers came through his village one day burning houses and killing the inhabitants. My friend, then a Muslim, was separated from his parents and had to flee immediately to save his life. He escaped to nearby Ethiopia and eventually was able to come to the United States. While a refugee in Ethiopia, he met several Christians who explained the gospel to him. Later he had dreams of someone delivering a message to him and asking him to read Jeremiah 29:12–13. He knew no Jeremiah and didn't know what the numbers meant. He later asked a friend, who had a Bible, if those words meant anything to him. He said yes, it was a passage in the Bible. The friend allowed him to read the passage, which, combined with some of his other dreams in which God was asking him to come to him, convinced him to surrender his life to God. He serves God diligently to this day, but the fate of his parents and siblings is still unknown. He was a seeker with little knowledge to whom God graciously gave more. There is no telling how God will respond to those who seek him. What we *can* believe is that he loves every person more than we ever would and will do all he can to bridge any gap for those with an earnest heart. This means those in heaven might be surprised at the persons they find dining with them at the heavenly banquet table!

God with Us

One of the hardest things to do in life is to go it alone. If there is a large task ahead and we are the only one to complete it, it can be overwhelming. If we try to do life alone it can feel just as overwhelming. So, many of us develop a group of friends that we form close bonds with. We get married to someone to be our mate for a lifetime. We have children and grandchildren. There are a few people we might call "loners," but if we look closely even they have people who support them. We seem to be social by nature. We depend on and enjoy other people. However, sometimes people disappoint us. Friends become cool to us, a marriage collapses, or the people at work become more competitive than cooperative. People we put our trust in become untrustworthy. That hurts. We are shy about trusting people again. Sometimes people give up and turn to the animal kingdom. My dog always love me, even if I'm in a bad mood. My cat crawls up on my lap every evening and purrs—what a comfort! They don't talk back, they don't argue, they listen, they lick my face; the perfect friend, right?

All of these life helpmates are good as far as they go, but they were never designed to be ultimate. They are secondary, and if we hang our ultimate trust on them we will be disappointed. Our primary relationship need has always been God. He has always wanted to be with us, and he will be as close as we let him. He was with Adam and Eve in the Garden of Eden. He shepherded the nation of Israel as his chosen people, never deserting them. They frequently walked away from him to serve idols of wood and metal, but he was ever faithful. He was tempted to abandon them, but never gave up on them. King David, leader of Israel, one of the most prolific psalmists, knew God was with him. Listen to his words from Psalm 23:

> *The Lord is my shepherd, I lack nothing. He makes me lie down in green pastures,*
> *he leads me beside quiet waters, he refreshes my soul.*
> *He guides me along the right paths for his name's sake.*
> *Even though I walk through the darkest valley I will fear no evil, for you are with me;*
> *your rod and your staff, they comfort me.*
> *You prepare a table before me in the presence of my enemies.*
> *You anoint my head with oil; my cup overflows.*
> *Surely your goodness and love will follow me all the days of my life,*
> *and I will dwell in the house of the Lord forever.* (Psalm 23)[32]

The greatest condescension of all, God came down to earth and became one of us, feeling our joys and pains and experiencing our temptations. He gave his life to save ours. So this being *with us* has gone on a long time. When Jesus came to earth one of his names was Emmanuel, which means "God with us" (Matt 1:23). When Jesus left, he and his Father gave the Holy Spirit, a member of the Trinity, to live inside us. He chooses to walk with those who will let him day by day. He is frequently not felt in an emotional way, but that does not diminish his presence. James reminds his fellow Christians that God will come near to us when we come near to him (Jas 4:8). Paul reminded Roman Christians that nothing could separate them from God's love:

---

32. Here are a couple contemporary Christian songs that proclaim that God is with us: People & Songs, "Psalm 23"; Austin Stone Worship, "Emmanuel God with Us." See the bibliography.

> *For I am convinced that neither death nor life, neither angels nor demons, neither the present nor the future, nor any powers, neither height nor depth, nor anything else in all creation, will be able to separate us from the love of God that is in Christ Jesus our Lord.* (Rom 8:38–39)

Jesus himself promised to be with his disciples, to include current ones, until the end:

> *Then Jesus came to them and said, "All authority in heaven and on earth has been given to me. Therefore go and make disciples of all nations, baptizing them in the name of the Father and of the Son and of the Holy Spirit, and teaching them to obey everything I have commanded you. And surely I am with you always, to the very end of the age."* (Matt 28:18–20)

And after the end of the age there is still more. God promises to be with us forever. To want to be with someone forever means there has to be a lot of love (Just consider what some of us are like!). But God's love is not in short supply. In what Christians call "heaven" and "the new heavens and earth,"[33] God will be *with us* forever.

So, the earthly reconciled life will have trials and sufferings. What is the consolation for the believer? It is *God with us* through it all. This is the answer to the question, "What in the world is God up to *with trying to reconcile us*?" He loves and wants to be *with us*! The *ultimate* consolation is *God with us forever*. We've occasionally mentioned heaven and Jesus' second coming to earth so far, which foretells that there is more to our destiny than this earthly life. The ultimate joy of being reconciled is to be with God forever in a much more revealing and intimate existence. But some see the Christian's hope of heaven as only wishful thinking, an attempted escape from reality, and as not confronting the difficulties of this present world. Tim Stafford gives us some good perspective:

> Rather than providing an escape from reality, the Second Coming clarifies the very nature of reality. Much of what we call "real" becomes insubstantial when seen in light of Jesus. What

---

33. There is a distinction in Christian theology between "heaven" and "the new heavens and earth." Up until Jesus returns to earth, which is called the second coming (this will be part of the topic of the next chapter), it seems after death God's followers from creation until now will be in a spiritual place called heaven, where people are consciously in God's presence. It is an intermediate state, with the final state to come. After Christ returns there is the final judgment, after which God will come down and make his permanent home with his people. This new heavens and earth will either be a renewed earth or a whole new one—it is hard to tell from the information we have. This is described in more detail in the last chapters of the book of Revelation.

will fame be worth for those whom the Everlasting One dismisses with, "Go away; I don't recognize you"? The enduring things will be those that have already the quality of heaven: love, and service, and especially adoration of the Lord . . .

Not only does this have very practical implications here and now, but it helps us as we deal with the question I have been discussing throughout this book: . . . How do we reconcile our longing for God with the dull facts of where we are [now]? Now we can see that we cannot reconcile it and ought not try. Our unfulfilled desire has a point: it will motivate us to care about living faithfully . . . Only those who ache to be with Jesus will do his will more, not less, as they wait for his arrival.

Here and now we do not have Jesus as we want to have him. But rather than trying to do away with our uncomfortable unfulfillment, we should let ourselves feel most deeply what we miss. We should allow ourselves to dream of Jesus' full presence as we prepare for his coming.

The Second Coming is not the end of history; it is the fulfillment of history—a history we are now making. The King is coming. Let the kingdom prepare.[34]

The coming of Christ again and the future that brings for the believer is our final topic, discussed now in chapter 4.

---

34. Stafford, *Knowing*, 223–24.

4

Restoration and Glory Forever

THERE IS A SONG from 1969 made popular by Peggy Lee titled "Is That All There Is?" It's a lilting, melancholy tune that expresses a disappointment and lack of satisfaction with life. The lyrics speak of events in a person's life that were difficult or underwhelming—a fire that destroys the house of a little girl, a big-tent circus, and falling in love for the first time. These disappointments lead to the chorus, which chimes that if this life is all there is, we might as well dance, drink, and have a ball. The question naturally surfaces that if that's the case, just end it all—commit suicide. But the lyrics end with a "no" to suicide, because death will likely be just as disappointing, so I'll keep living for now. There are other reasons people value this life only—it's short, so live it up now for tomorrow we may die (Isa 22:13)! Or, "I'm doing so well and prospering that I don't have to worry about the future. Take it easy, eat, drink, be merry!" (Luke 12:19, the parable of the rich fool). Behind them all is the idea that this life is all there is, and if it's a downer, too short, or too good, we better either give up or celebrate before anything deadly happens. These are the choices for those without God. But there is a hint in our song that gives away something. "Is That All There Is?" tells us that the singer knows there is more, wants there to be more, but can't find it. The apostle Paul realized these questions and told his fellow Christians that if Christ was not raised from the dead then neither are they raised. Their faith and hope are futile. We are still in our sins. He closes, "If only for this life we have hope in Christ, we are of all people most to be pitied" (1 Cor 15:19). If you remember we discussed that we are in a spiritual battle, Christian or not. Satan, the devil, is a deceiver (1 Pet 5:8; 2 Cor 11:14; Eph 6:11–12; John 8:43–45). He'd like to convince us that heaven doesn't exist. If he can't do that, he'll whisper that it's not a place anyone would want to go—playing harps and sitting on clouds. It would all be rather boring.

The good news is that none of these ideas are true. There *is* more than our physical existence—and better—beyond even the best things we can imagine. If we know the Creator of life we will spend eternity with him and the rest of our brothers and sisters in the faith. And this is just like God, who is the expert at renewing things. Think of the words we have used already regarding how God works for good: reconcile, redeem, restore, return (repent), renew, regenerate, resurrect.

THE CURRENT HEAVEN

The beginning of God's renewal process is the current heaven. It is a wonderful place. Those there are conscious and enjoy the presence of God and all his followers who have died up to this point. Randy Alcorn summarizes the process:

> "The dust returns to the ground it came from, and the spirit returns to God who gave it" (Ecclesiastes 12:7). At death, the human spirit goes either to Heaven or Hell. Christ depicted Lazarus and the rich man as conscious in Heaven and Hell immediately after they died (Luke 17:22–31). Jesus told the dying thief on the cross, "Today you will be with me in paradise" (Luke 23:43). The apostle Paul said that to die was to be with Christ (Philippians 1:23), and to be absent from the body was to be present with the Lord (2 Corinthians 5:8). After their death, martyrs are pictured in Heaven, crying out to God to bring justice on Earth (Revelation 6:9–11) . . . The spirit's departure from the body ends our existence on Earth. The physical part of us "sleeps" until the resurrection, while the spiritual part of us relocates to a conscious existence in Heaven (Daniel 12:2–3; 2 Corinthians 5:8).[1]

Again, this is an intermediate state, and the Christian awaits a new resurrected body that will be able to live forever on the new earth. Will there be plants and animals in this intermediate state? Will we eat, harvest crops, work, do sports, paint pictures, play music, and do other things that we think of as common on this earth? What will existence be like before we are reunited with our resurrected bodies? Unfortunately our knowledge of those answers is limited. What we do know more about is what comes next.

1. Alcorn, *Heaven*, 46–47.

THE TRANSITION

Out of all the "re-" words we've just summarized the words most relevant for the future of God's people and the world are "restore" and "resurrect." God will destroy/remake the current world and bring forth a restored world. It will be glorious! God's people will be resurrected to acquire new bodies that will live forever. God has revealed that there will be a certain timeline in which these things will come about. There is some disagreement on the details, but the main events are clear. Christ promised to return to this earth, an event frequently called the Second Coming (Acts 1:10–11; Rev 1:7; 1 Thess 4:16–17). Those who have died in the faith will be called forth by Christ to join him as he comes down to greet those believers who are still alive on earth. Just before or just after this (this is where there is some disagreement) there will be a seven-year time of great trouble on the earth, called the Great Tribulation. This will include the reign of the Antichrist, great judgments on those not worshipping God, epic military battles, and the final battle of Armageddon. This is followed by the judgment of Satan, who will be cast into the lake of fire forever.[2] Next will be the Great White Throne Judgment (Rev 20:11–15), in which humans are judged by what they have done in this life. Those who loved God supremely, who had their names written in the book of life, will live with God and each other forever. Those not found in the book will be cast into the lake of fire. Following this the new heavens and earth will become a reality. John, in the book of Revelation, describes it as the new Jerusalem, the Holy City, descending from heaven and from God:

> *I saw the Holy City, the new Jerusalem, coming down out of heaven from God, prepared as a bride beautifully dressed for her husband. And I heard a loud voice from the throne saying, "Look! God's dwelling place is now among the people, and he will dwell with them. They will be his people, and God himself will be with them and be their God. He will wipe every tear from their eyes. There will be no more death or mourning or crying or pain, for the old order of things has passed away." He who was seated on the throne said, "I am making everything new!"* (Rev 21:2–5; see also Isa 65:17)

So the new heavens and earth are the final abode of the righteous, and God will live with them forever. As we discussed earlier, those who die now as Christians will go to the intermediate state of "heaven" and will await the final redemption of their bodies at Christ's second coming.

---

2. The lake of fire is the final abode for Satan, demons, and all humans who have followed his ways. It is for all those whose names were not written in the book of life. You could call it the final hell.

Christians eagerly look forward to that day when they will be with the ones they loved—the Father, Son, and Holy Spirit. The apostle Paul encouraged Colossian believers to set their mind on heavenly things, to live in anticipation of that day (Col 3:1). That anticipation had a this-worldly benefit—their hope of heaven birthed the faith and love they currently showed to their fellow saints (Col 1:5). However, this world is not their ultimate home. Christ's followers, just like the saints of old, should and do long for a "better country." In truth they knew they were aliens and strangers on earth (Heb 11:16). Why do Christians look forward to something they haven't experienced yet? Because even in the OT the writer of Ecclesiastes knew that God had set eternity in the human heart (Eccl 3:1). We long to be home, to the place we were always meant to be.

WHAT WILL THE NEW HEAVENS AND EARTH BE LIKE?

The new heavens and earth is certainly a place, but likely not exactly like our current physical existence. It has been referred to as a country, a city, a house, and where there will be nations. Jesus said he went to prepare a place for his followers and that his father's house had many rooms (John 14:1–2). It will likely be a restored earth, an earth like the original Garden of Eden, except more extensive. Words escape us at this point—but it will be better! The angel told John the Revelator that this new earth will contain a new Jerusalem, which will have a jasper wall around it with twelve gates and twelve angels attending them. Each gate will be a huge pearl, each with a name of one of the twelve tribes of Israel. These gates will be always open. The foundation of the city will be made of twelve layers of precious stones, each one with a name of one of the twelve apostles. The wall will be two hundred feet thick and the dimensions of the city form a cube 1400 miles per side. The streets will be of gold that look like pure glass. There will be no temple because the Father and the Son will be the temple and its source of light. The glories and wonders of all kings and their nations will be brought into it. The crystal-clear river of life will flow through it, and the tree of life will be on both sides, yielding twelve crops of fruit, one per month. Whatever redeemable things that the nations of the earth bring into it the tree of life will heal and make whole. The Father and Son's thrones will be in the city, and their servants will serve and reign with them (Rev 21–22). Some count this description as figurative and some as literal. Sometimes we limit God to the things we can conceive of or have experienced. Either way it will be God's best.

We know this is good news because we know what our current world is like, and it's not in good shape. Even as Christians, there is groaning and suffering. Paul describes what's coming:

> *I consider that our present sufferings are not worth comparing with the glory that will be revealed in us. For the creation waits in eager expectation for the children of God to be revealed. For the creation was subjected to frustration, not by its own choice, but by the will of the one who subjected it, in hope that the creation itself will be liberated from its bondage to decay and brought into the freedom and glory of the children of God.*
>
> *We know that the whole creation has been groaning as in the pains of childbirth right up to the present time. Not only so, but we ourselves, who have the firstfruits of the Spirit, groan inwardly as we wait eagerly for our adoption to sonship, the redemption of our bodies. For in this hope we were saved. But hope that is seen is no hope at all. Who hopes for what they already have? But if we hope for what we do not yet have, we wait for it patiently.* (Rom 8:18–25)

This means the Christian's resurrection to a new existence with a spiritual body is linked to the renewal of the whole cosmos, the whole universe! What will be made better? Everything! Mountains, prairies, forests, rivers, lakes, oceans, plants, animals, stars, galaxies—everything! Remember, it's a new heavens as well as a new earth—everything in our sky (the universe) will be made new. Maybe we'll be able to visit other planets or travel to other galaxies. How will our earth be made better? We don't know. But the earth will be the best, the most beautiful and safest it has ever been. I don't see floods, drought, hurricanes, tornadoes, tsunamis, or unbearable heat or cold as being a part of it. Here is where the Christian can use some redeemed imagination. Imagine the ultimate earth and universe—what would it be like? And what will God reveal that we've never seen before that will drop our jaw?

Beyond nature, we know there will be at least one big city, the new Jerusalem. Will there be other cities? Will the good things about our current earthly cultures translate over? Will all the good things humankind has made be allowed in—in art, music, architecture, science? No one is sure, but I would bet so. It seems like God would do such a thing.

Looking more personally, what will the believer's new body be like? It sounds like it will be material. Paul said Christians would have a spiritual "body," not that they would be "spirits" (1 Cor 15:44). In his letter to the Philippian believers Paul said, "But our citizenship is in heaven. And we eagerly await a Savior from there, the Lord Jesus Christ, who, by the power that enables him to bring everything under his control, will transform our lowly bodies so that they will be like his glorious body" (Phil 3:20–21). Whatever form it takes, it will be better than our current one. After all, it will last forever. It won't become sick. Whatever imperfections it had on earth will be gone. If you were blind, you can see. If you were paralyzed, you can walk, and run! Everything about us that needed any healing will be healed; we will be whole. Maybe we can even fly, who knows! I'm imagining here—maybe we can go to other planets and visit (even better than *Star Trek* and Scotty beaming me up). I'd like to.

How about our relationships? Think of all the redeemed people we'll meet. It would take forever to know them all (and we'll have it!). Who will we be able to talk to? Everyone! And they'll all be good. No jealousy, power-seeking, ulterior motives, envy, boasting, pride, rudeness, anger, revenge, or laziness (I'm borrowing from 1 Corinthians 13 here). They'll love us and we'll love them. Further, I can't imagine us not talking to angels and hearing their stories.

Will our current good relationships be maintained? It appears marriage will be unnecessary, and our current mates will not be our mates in heaven (Matt 22:30). One of the functions of marriage is to procreate, and that function will not be needed. We will surely know our mates and our children and other relatives who are there, but all our relationship needs will be met by God himself and all of our beloved fellow believers. There will be no loneliness, for every being that can satisfy our desire for love and companionship will be there.

What Will We Do on the New Earth?

One of the most satisfying things we experience with someone we love is to just "be" with them. We don't have to do anything in particular. Lovers just want to look into each other's eyes. Maybe have an intimate conversation as they walk along a riverbank. As we've said, the best part of the new earth will be enjoying God. God will actually "dwell" with us (Rev 21:3-4). We will be transformed by being with God. We will see him face to face. The apostle John says to the churches, "Dear friends, now we are children of God, and what we will be has not yet been made known. But we know that when Christ appears, we shall be like him, for we shall see him as he is" (1 John 3:2). Paul tells the Corinthian believers about meeting God after they die, "For now we see only a reflection as in a mirror; then we shall see face to face. Now I know in part; then I shall know fully, even as I am fully known" (1 Cor 13:12). The greatest blessing will be talking with the Trinity. Can you imagine talking to the Father about creating the universe, or to Jesus about his life on earth, or to the Holy Spirit about how he worked in people's lives? Will you thank the Father for sending his son, thank the Holy Spirit for helping you become more Christlike? Thank Jesus for sacrificing himself for you? Will you walk with Jesus along a mountain path and discuss everything that he has planned for you? Will you sing songs of praise with a choir of millions? The answer to the last question is a definite yes—when we see God face to face there can only be one appropriate response—worship! Here it is best to quote what the creatures and people of heaven saw and did as they beheld the Father and Son (the Lamb slain for them):

> *And they sang a new song, saying:*
>   *"You are worthy to take the scroll*
>   *and to open its seals,*
>   *because you were slain,*
>   *and with your blood you purchased for God*
>   *persons from every tribe and language and people and nation.*
>   *You have made them to be a kingdom and priests to serve our God,*
>   *and they will reign on the earth."*
> *Then I looked and heard the voice of many angels, numbering thousands upon thousands, and ten thousand times ten thousand. They encircled the throne and the living creatures and the elders. In a loud voice they were saying:*
>   *"Worthy is the Lamb, who was slain,*
>   *to receive power and wealth and wisdom and strength*
>   *and honor and glory and praise!"*
> *Then I heard every creature in heaven and on earth and under the earth and on the sea, and all that is in them, saying:*
>   *"To him who sits on the throne and to the Lamb*
>   *be praise and honor and glory and power,*
>   *for ever and ever!"* (Rev 5:9–13)

Those kind of words give the Christian goosebumps! Briefly mentioned in these songs is the idea of reigning. Jesus also mentioned his twelve apostles sitting on thrones and judging the twelve tribes of Israel (Luke 12:30) and hinted that his disciples would rule—even cities—on the new earth (Luke 19:17), to include people and angels (1 Cor 6:2–3). This sounds like a recreating of our original roles, given to Adam and Eve, to rule and subdue the earth (Gen 1:26–28). Some may balk at the responsibility of ruling, but this will be a redeemed ruling:

> Imagine responsibility, service, and leadership that's pure joy. The responsibility that God will entrust to us as a reward can only be good for us, and we'll find delight in it. To rule on the

New Earth will be to enable, equip and guide, offering wisdom and encouragement to those under our authority. We've so often seen leadership twisted that we've lost a biblical view of what ruling, or exercising dominion, really means. God, ruler of the universe, is living proof that ruling can and should be good.[3]

Governing is not a necessity because of sin. God governs, and God gave Adam and Eve the task to rule before they sinned. But many of us may just be followers. Whatever our job, it will fit who we are.

If we *have* other jobs, they will be fulfilling and help God's kingdom flourish. Work is a good thing; menial work will not exist. Everything we do will bring about some noticeable good. In the beginning Adam tended the Garden of Eden God made. Our work will be something we enjoy, and who knows who we will do it with:

> Maybe you'll build a cabinet with Joseph of Nazareth. Or with Jesus. Maybe you'll tend sheep with David, discuss medicine with Luke, sew with Dorcas, make clothes with Lydia, design a new tent with Paul or Priscilla, write a song with Isaac Watts, ride horses with John Wesley, or sing with Keith Green. Maybe you'll write a theology of the Trinity, bouncing your thoughts off Paul, John, Polycarp, Cyprian, Augustine, Calvin, Wesley . . . and even Jesus.[4]

Looking outward, we may manage planets or star systems or galaxies. Maybe we'll colonize them. Again, I'm just imagining. If none of that is true, it will be something better.

What follows work? Rest. Play. Recreating. Eating. Whatever is good here will be redeemed and better there. Eating is specifically implied and mentioned. Jesus ate in his resurrected body (Luke 24:40–43). There will be feasting (Matt 8:11) and drinking (Matt 26:29). It all sounds good to me.

Going Home

After all the work Christians will do, it will be nice to be home. "Home" is probably one of the best words to describe our new earth and it will certainly feel like the ultimate home. We will recognize it because it will still be earth, but remade. We will relax there and be at peace. Randy Alcorn gives us a feel of how we can anticipate it and why we ache for it:

---

3. Alcorn, *Heaven*, 220–21.
4. Alcorn, *Heaven*, 332–33.

Do you recall a time when you were away from your earthly home and desperately missed it? Maybe it was when you were off at college or in the military or traveling extensively overseas or needed to move because of a job. Do you remember how your heart ached for home? That's how we should feel about Heaven. We are a displaced people, longing for our home. C. S. Lewis said, "If I find myself a desire which no experience in this world can satisfy, the most probable explanation is that I was made for another world" . . .

Nothing is more often misdiagnosed than our homesickness for Heaven. We think that what we want is sex, drugs, alcohol, a new job, a raise, a doctorate, a spouse, a large-screen television, a new car, a cabin in the woods, a condo in Hawaii. What we really want is the person we were made for, Jesus, and the place we were made for, Heaven. Nothing less can satisfy us.[5]

Maybe an analogy will make it more real:

In *The Happiness of Heaven*, published in 1871, Father J. Boudreau tells of a kindhearted king who finds a blind, destitute orphan boy while hunting in a forest. The king takes the boy to his palace, adopts him as his son, and provides for his care. He sees that the boy receives the finest education. The boy is extremely grateful and he loves the king, his new father, with all his heart.

When the boys turns twenty, a surgeon performs an operation on his eyes, and for the first time he is able to see.

This boy, once a starving orphan, has for some years been a royal prince, at home in the king's palace. But something wonderful has happened, something far greater than the magnificent food, gardens, libraries, music, and wonders of the palace. The boy is finally able to *see* the father he loves. Boudreau writes, "I will not attempt to describe the joys that will overwhelm the soul of this fortunate young man when he first sees that king, of whose manly beauty, goodness, power, and magnificence he has heard so much. Nor will I attempt to describe the other joys which fill his soul when he beholds his own personal beauty, and the magnificence of his princely garments whereof he had also heard so much heretofore. Much less will I attempt to picture his exquisite and unspeakable happiness when he sees himself adopted into the royal family, honored and loved by all, together with all the pleasures of life within his reach . . . All this taken together is a beatific vision for him."[6]

5. Alcorn, *Heaven*, 166.
6. Alcorn, *Heaven*, 180–81. A beatific vision is when a person is able to see God in

God wants to share his glory with us.* Jesus prayed to his Father before he was crucified and asked that his followers would be able to be with him and to see his glory (John 17:24). On the new earth he will see his prayer fulfilled. We will be home with our Savior.

Rewards

The Bible writers and Jesus himself talked about rewards in heaven. It seems that believers will be looked at by God and given various rewards for their life of love and service. All who are believers who prevail under trial will receive the "crown of life," promised to those who love God (Jas 1:12; 2 Tim 4:8). It is part of the Christian's inheritance (Col 3:24). Paul reminded the Romans that those who persist in doing good will receive glory, honor, and immortality (Rom 2:6–7). Beyond that, the apostle Paul uses the analogy of constructing a building to say that what any Christian "builds" for God on this earth will be revealed on the "day" of judgment. How was our love toward God? What did we do that showed that? Did we serve God with all our hearts and our fellow humans as ourselves? Did we do things sacrificially with our talents, our time, our resources (think of the meaning of *agape* love)? A review of the "love" chapter of 1 Corinthians 13 will give us perspective on ourselves. Works that pleased God, when tested by the great heat of a refining fire, will come out well, like gold, silver, or precious jewels. Inferior work will be burned up by such a fire and will be destroyed, even though the person will be saved, just missing the flames (1 Cor 3:10–16). In a letter to Timothy Paul reminds him that it is the one who is rich in good works that is truly living, and will store up treasure for himself (1 Tim 1:12). Jesus said that those who suffer and are persecuted because of him will receive a *great* reward (Matt 5:11–12). He added that giving sacrificially to the poor, loving our enemies, and lending without expecting repayment also results in treasure and reward (Matt 19:21; Luke 6:25). Christians will be given the appropriate recompense for their deeds (Matt 16:27). The idea of rewards is furthered by the parable of the talents. This parable shows that Jesus is looking for faithfulness. The one who buried the resources God gave him was condemned. Those who used what they had, whatever their gifts were and to whatever degree, were blessed. They were given great responsibility for their faithfulness. Another aspect of reward, joy, is highlighted by Paul. He reminds Thessalonian believers that part of their reward will be the joy of seeing others come to salvation, especially if we were instrumental in the process (1 Thess 2:19–20).

---

all his glory, as much as is possible for us humans.

The exact nature of God's rewards is hinted at, like joy or responsibilities we relish in, but the nature or quantity of them should not be our concern. God's followers do not serve him for some extraneous reward; it is never held out as a top priority. Rewards are a byproduct, not a prime product. The greatest reward is being on the new earth with the Savior we loved and all those who followed him. Anything else that God wants to bless us with we'll receive with humble gratitude.

CONCLUSION

This chapter has been the shortest, and for good reason. There is a lot we don't know about the details. There are hundreds of questions we could ask, but there are few definitive answers.[7] In this chapter I've used words like "imagine," "likely," "probably," and "hint." I think my guesses are good, but I can not guarantee them. If they turn out wrong, then God has planned something different, something that will be just right for our future existence with him. That's something we can be sure of. And the answer to the question of our book, "What in the world is God up to in *creating heaven and the new heavens and earth*?" is a ditto from the last chapter. He wants to be *with us*, and the almost unbelievable follow-up is that he wants to be with us *forever*:

> And I heard a loud voice from the throne saying, "Look! God's dwelling place is now among the people, and he will dwell with them. They will be his people, and God himself will be with them and be their God. He will wipe every tear from their eyes. There will be no more death or mourning or crying or pain, for the old order of things has passed away." (Rev 21:3–4)

---

7. A book I've quoted from a lot in this chapter is Randy Alcorn's *Heaven*. He has done a lot of research, but there are just as many "likelys" and "probablys" in his book, too. He goes into more detail in answering tentatively many of the questions you might have. Give it a look. Additionally, Lee Strobel has come out with one of his The Case for . . . books on heaven. It gives a good defense for the existence of heaven, the new heavens and earth, and the traditional concept of hell. He and his experts describe it much the way we have in this book. Well worth reading.

5

Conclusion

We've covered a lot of ground. There are whole Christian books that cover only one of our chapters or one particular topic. That's okay—our goal was to provide a summary of God's plan and what he is trying to accomplish with us. So, has the question of our title been answered? Can we see the big picture? I think so. God is behind everything we see, he loves us, has given us freedom, has sacrificed much to remedy our transgressions, and has big plans for our future. We questioned whether God is adequately supervising this mixture of good and evil we see on our planet. Because of the nature of our freedom, he does not intervene in every case of impending evil. He watches, tests, encourages good, punishes evil in limited ways now but will ultimately sequester all that is evil away from all that is good. Sometimes we want all of life's injustices prevented or rectified now, but God is patiently waiting for those who do not love him to change their minds. The apostle Peter reminds us about the timing of Christ's return and making all things right: "The Lord is not slow in keeping his promise, as some understand slowness. Instead he is patient with you, not wanting anyone to perish, but everyone to come to repentance" (2 Pet 3:9). Our desire for clear answers from God on important issues is also sometimes unmet. As we discussed, many times God is subtle, giving us enough information to trust him but not the whole picture. That is left up to his wisdom. He also tests, watching to see what we will do with situations that challenge our faith. And why aren't Christians more holy with less struggle? It seems God has the same question. God revealing himself more fully doesn't really help in that regard.

Remember the nation of Israel? They had great revelations of God's presence and power but it did not produce any more devotion. In the end he only expects of us what we can deliver. Also, we humans tend to take things for granted. Give us too much revelation or power and we tend to forget the Giver. God wants to keep us close to him, and we need to be reminded often that we are dependent; we are creatures, not God.

We've seen David, king over Israel, one who rose to great spiritual heights and fell to great spiritual depths. He was courageous, generous, patient, lustful, devious, and neglectful as a parent. God lauded his devotion but also punished his sins. David had many questions for God, as we sometimes do. He wrote many of the Psalms, and he frequently questioned God in them: "How long, O Lord, will you hide your face from me?" "Why do my enemies triumph over me?" "Do you judge rightly among men?" "When will you come to me?" But in the end he saw God's big picture. He ended up trusting and praising God because he knew God's heart. Read his Psalm 103:

> *Praise the Lord, my soul;*
> > *all my inmost being, praise his holy name.*
> *Praise the* Lord, *my soul,*
> > *and forget not all his benefits—*
> *who forgives all your sins*
> > *and heals all your diseases,*
> *who redeems your life from the pit*
> > *and crowns you with love and compassion,*
> *who satisfies your desires with good things*
> > *so that your youth is renewed like the eagle's.*
> *The* Lord *works righteousness*
> > *and justice for all the oppressed.*
> *He made known his ways to Moses,*
> > *his deeds to the people of Israel:*
> *The* Lord *is compassionate and gracious,*
> > *slow to anger, abounding in love.*
> *He will not always accuse,*
> > *nor will he harbor his anger forever;*
> *he does not treat us as our sins deserve*
> > *or repay us according to our iniquities.*
> *For as high as the heavens are above the earth,*
> > *so great is his love for those who fear him;*
> *as far as the east is from the west,*
> > *so far has he removed our transgressions from us.*
> *As a father has compassion on his children,*
> > *so the* Lord *has compassion on those who fear him;*

> for he knows how we are formed,
> > he remembers that we are dust.
> The life of mortals is like grass,
> > they flourish like a flower of the field;
> the wind blows over it and it is gone,
> > and its place remembers it no more.
> But from everlasting to everlasting
> > the LORD's love is with those who fear him,
> > and his righteousness with their children's children—
> with those who keep his covenant
> > and remember to obey his precepts.
> The LORD has established his throne in heaven,
> > and his kingdom rules over all.
> Praise the LORD, you his angels,
> > you mighty ones who do his bidding,
> > who obey his word.
> Praise the LORD, all his heavenly hosts,
> > you his servants who do his will.
> Praise the LORD, all his works
> > everywhere in his dominion.
> Praise the Lord, my soul.

What comforting and inspiring words!

I mentioned in the Introduction that I was writing to several audiences. If you are not a Christian, then I hope this book has given you a picture of God's plan and his heart. He loves you and wants to know you. He wants you to give up things that are unworthy of him and yourself. He wants your heart. He is your Creator and has designed you to only be whole in him. Respond in repentance and humility, and he will receive you. The apostle John received a revelation from Jesus Christ while on the island of Patmos. His closing words here in the last book of the Bible are appropriate for you as we look at where history is headed:

> "Look, I am coming soon! My reward is with me, and I will give to each person according to what they have done. I am the Alpha and the Omega, the First and the Last, the Beginning and the End.
>
> "Blessed are those who wash their robes, that they may have the right to the tree of life and may go through the gates into the city. Outside are the dogs, those who practice magic arts, the sexually immoral, the murderers, the idolaters and everyone who loves and practices falsehood.
>
> "I, Jesus, have sent my angel to give you this testimony for the churches. I am the Root and the Offspring of David, and the bright Morning Star."

> *The Spirit and the bride say, "Come!" And let the one who hears say, "Come!" Let the one who is thirsty come; and let the one who wishes take the free gift of the water of life.* (Rev 22:12-17)

For you who are already Christians, I hope this has been helpful—that you understand the God you serve better. I hope you see more clearly where he is going in history and with your own life. May that comfort your soul and give you important things you can share with those who ask you, "What in the world is God up to?" I think these words from the apostle Peter are appropriate for you:

> *Praise be to the God and Father of our Lord Jesus Christ! In his great mercy he has given us new birth into a living hope through the resurrection of Jesus Christ from the dead, and into an inheritance that can never perish, spoil or fade. This inheritance is kept in heaven for you, who through faith are shielded by God's power until the coming of the salvation that is ready to be revealed in the last time. In all this you greatly rejoice, though now for a little while you may have had to suffer grief in all kinds of trials. These have come so that the proven genuineness of your faith—of greater worth than gold, which perishes even though refined by fire—may result in praise, glory and honor when Jesus Christ is revealed. Though you have not seen him, you love him; and even though you do not see him now, you believe in him and are filled with an inexpressible and glorious joy, for you are receiving the end result of your faith, the salvation of your souls.* (1 Pet 1:3-9)

Amen.

Appendix A: A Brief Apology

THE QUESTION OF WHAT the God of the Bible is up to in this world assumes certain facts. First, it assumes there is a Supreme First Cause that has generated this world, us, and everything else in the universe. Second, it presumes that the God of the Bible exists as this Supreme First Cause and that the description of the Trinity and the Trinity's relationship to the world and humanity is truthful and accurate. Those are assumptions that are beyond most of the scope of this book. There are many scholars who address these assumptions, and their books defend them. Some have been referenced, mostly in the footnotes. However, we will dip our toes into the water a little to at least set the stage for our discussion.

First, we assume there is a Supreme Cause. When we look at the universe we inhabit, we can reasonably ask why there is anything at all—anything referring to the physical universe and specifically to our own world of the earth, its plants, animals, and us. We have also discovered that our universe is controlled by laws in physics, chemistry, thermodynamics and every other physical and biological science. Why is the universe governed by laws at all? Why isn't everything just random? Why is there not just "nothing"? Why is there time? Why are the physical constants of the universe just right for matter and life to exist (if these constants were minutely different, there would be no universe)? Relatedly, why is the earth in just the right place in our galaxy with just the right size sun, just the right distance from that sun, just the right size with just the right proportion of water and land mass, tilted at just the right angle, with just the right kind of atmosphere to shelter life from harmful rays from the sun and outer space? The evidence suggests our whole existence is not by chance, not random, but intentional. Intent comes from something that can form intent, like a Supreme Cause or Being.

Further, when we look to the universe, we discover that all physical events have causes. Physical matter and all the events that affect it only change as a result of causes. So if we go backward, logically and in time, there must be a first cause. Some say the universe just popped into existence without a cause. Random "quantum singularities" just began to exist, and these are described by scientists as "nothing" and as the building blocks of the universe. However, if they have a name, then they are "something!" Evidence suggests the physical universe had a beginning in a very small but very dense "something" that exploded. This explosion scientists call the Big Bang. However, they have no credible idea where this initial stuff came from. The universe did not self-create. It seems the best explanation is that our universe came about from a source that is beyond the physical. A spiritual and very powerful first cause seems very likely.

Second, we conclude the God of the Bible is this first cause. When we look around we see there are many candidates for a spiritual first cause. The world religions describe first causes (or no causes at all) and include Hinduism, Buddhism, Islam, Judaism, Christianity, many folk religions, Chinese, Japanese, and Native American religions. Why should we favor Christianity as the best option since some would say there is a core commonality among all these—love? If we love our fellow human beings and even ourselves, that is the core of all religions. Other virtues, such as kindness, justice, mercy, compassion, impartiality, peacefulness, and self-sacrifice are frequently added in. Just pick which religion fits you best, strive for these virtues, and that is all that is required. This model is sometimes illustrated by several blind men discovering an elephant. One says it is like a long, swishy, and hairy rod (a tail), four say it is like a leathery tree (a leg), a third says it is smooth, hard, long, and comes to a point (a tusk), and the last says it is like a thick leathery snake with a wet end (a trunk). In the end they are all describing the same thing—an elephant! The problem is—how did this all-seeing-eye person get the perspective that all these descriptions are an elephant? The analogy fails.

By looking closer we see that all these religious attempts to explain the universe and our life in it are not the same. Yes, many of them hold high the value of love, but do they give us the power to love unselfishly? Further, there are significant differences. The god or gods they describe are different in being and behavior. In some God is personal, in others there is no personal god or no god at all, and in still others the gods have different personalities. In some we are made like God, in others we are actually part of God. This obviously affects how we relate to and communicate with the divine, if that is even possible. With some angels and demons exist; in others they don't. In some there is a personal, conscious hereafter; in others there is no discreet consciousness after this life. Some give persons many lifetimes to become more perfect; in others this one earthly life is the first part of a second hereafter. They disagree on whether we can trust our senses. How we are to acquire religious knowledge differs—is it through impressions, direct divine contact, prayer, a sacred book, ritual? The actual ethical and behavioral standards they ask of followers are different (For instance, is violence a viable way to make converts? How are we to treat our enemies or those of other faiths? How should we treat animals and the physical world? How should husbands, wives, and children interact?). How the universe came to be is described differently.

So, in the end we need to compare, and we need to decide on what criteria to compare with. Philosophy can help us in this regard since it has come up with helpful criteria for comparing ideas and theories, irrespective of their source. There is the concept of "inference to the best explanation," which asks which idea or theory presents the best cumulative case for whatever is being described. Its criteria include:

- *Explanatory power and scope*—Does it explain the wide range of human experience and all interactions with the world and the divine well? Are there things it assumes are unexplainable that other religions can explain? Can it explain good and bad human behavior?
- *Logical consistency*—Which explanation best follows the laws of logic, which apply to all human thinking and communication? Does it break any consistently?
- *Coherence*—Does this religion exude internal consistency among its beliefs, or are there contradictions it leaves unanswered?
- *Less ad hoc*—Does it require makeshift or extraneous assumptions or explanations to avoid contradictions?
- *Ability to integrate*—Does it successfully integrate knowledge from psychology, sociology, the physical sciences, biology, and history?
- *Existential viability*—Can adherents live like the religion says they should live? Does it allow adherents to cope with life's challenges and to exhibit obvious flourishing? Does it give adherents the power to make positive change? Does it meet the human pre-loaded need to love and be loved by the god(s) and adherents? Does it offer norms/ethics that create human flourishing?

When these criteria are used, it seems Christianity does the best job of describing the way things "are," the best way for humans to behave and interact, and the best way to create a flourishing person and society. If one asked the questions, "If all the world followed this religion, what would be the result? Would individuals flourish and have their deepest needs met? Would neighbors get along? Would families love each other and work as a unit? Would nations live in peace beside each other? Would the physical world, plants, and animals flourish? Does it offer a real relationship with the divine?," then I think a world of Christians who have God's life inside them and who followed the teachings of Christ would produce the best result.

Bibliography

Alcorn, Randy. *Heaven*. Carol Stream, IL: Tyndale House, 2004.
Arnold, Clinton E. *3 Crucial Questions on Spiritual Warfare*. Grand Rapids: Baker Academic, 1997.
Austin Stone Worship. "Emmanuel God with Us." *YouTube*, November 17, 2017. https://www.youtube.com/watch?v=wIgAKkAaMKM.
BBC News. "Nigeria Kidnap: Gunmen Seize 140 Schoolchildren in Kaduna State." July 5, 2021. https://www.bbc.com/news/world-africa-57636851.
Blake, John. "When Exorcists Need Help, They Call Him." *CNN Health*, August 4, 2017. https://www.cnn.com/2017/08/04/health/exorcism-doctor/index.html.
Blomberg, Craig L. *The Historical Reliability of the New Testament*. Nashville: B. & H. Academic, 2016.
Brand, Paul, and Philip Yancey. *Fearfully and Wonderfully Made: The Marvel of Bearing God's Image*. Downers Grove: IVP Books, 2019.
———. *In His Image*. Grand Rapids: Zondervan, 1984.
Bright, Bill. *Have You Heard of the Four Spiritual Laws?* Peachtree, GA: Campus Crusade for Christ, 2007.
Bussey, Peter. *Signposts to God: How Modern Physics & Astronomy Point the Way to Belief*. Downers Grove: InterVarsity, 2016.
Christensen, Michael M. *God, Adam, and You: How Original Sin, the Flesh, and Holiness Integrate in the Christian Life*. Eugene, OR: Wipf & Stock, 2015.
Clayton, John. *The Source: Creation—Eternal Design or Infinite Accident?* West Monroe, LA: Howard, 2001.
Corduan, Winfried. *Neighboring Faiths: A Christian Introduction to World Religions*. Downers Grove: IVP Academic, 2012.
Dembski, William A., and James M. Kushiner, eds. *Signs of Intelligence: Understanding Intelligent Design*. Grand Rapids: Brazos, 2001.
DeYoung, Kevin. "Temptation Is Not the Same as Sin." *The Gospel Coalition*, September 26, 2013. https://www.thegospelcoalition.org/blogs/kevin-deyoung/temptation-is-not-the-same-as-sin/.
Dickson, John. *Bullies and Saints: An Honest Look at the Good and Evil of Christian History*. Grand Rapids: Zondervan, 2021.
DJimmytst. "The Dance of Love: Perichoresis." https://musicanddancing.wordpress.com/perichoresis.
Erickson, Millard J. *Christian Theology*. 2nd ed. Grand Rapids: Baker Academic, 1998.
Gammie, John. *Holiness in Israel*. Minneapolis: Fortress, 1989.

Hansen, Brant. *Blessed Are the Misfits*. Nashville: W Publishing Group, 2017.

Harvey, Dean H. *Ransom: The High Cost of Sin*. Maitland, FL: Xulon, 2010.

Jabakhanji, Sara. "London Man Saves Family of 4 'All Drowning Simultaneously' at Ontario Beach." *CBC News*, August 6, 2021. https://www.cbc.ca/news/canada/london/london-man-saves-mississauga-family-of-four-grand-bend-drowning-1.6130965.

Kitchen, K. A. *On the Reliability of the Old Testament*. Grand Rapids: Eerdmans, 2003.

Kolodiejchuk, Brian, ed. *Mother Theresa: Come Be My Light*. New York: Doubleday, 2007.

Kreeft, Peter, ed. *Christianity for Modern Pagans: Pascal's Pensées*. San Francisco: Ignatius, 1993.

Kruger, C. Baxter. *The Great Dance*. Vancouver, BC: Regent College Publishing, 2005.

Lewis, C. S. *Mere Christianity*. New York: Simon & Schuster, 1996.

———. *The Screwtape Letters*. New York: Simon & Schuster, 1996.

Lipka, Michael. "A Closer Look at American's Rapidly Growing Religious 'Nones.'" *Pew Research Center*, May 13, 2015. https://www.pewresearch.org/fact-tank/2015/05/13/a-closer-look-at-americas-rapidly-growing-religious-nones.

McDowell, Josh. "Is the Bible Reliable." https://www.josh.org/resurrection/is-the-bible-reliable/?mwm_id=241874010218&mot=J79GNF&gclid=CjwKCAjw87SHBhBiE iwAukSeUWHcRKrQ7K52uto6bqRbHzg-8VqPZ8X4N9qdSGjrqFEHU53S6wclr hoCBJEQAvD_BwE.

McGee, Robert S. *The Search for Significance*. Nashville: W Publishing Group, 2003.

Messages of Christ. "Solomon's Temple Explained." *YouTube*, July 19, 2018. https://www.youtube.com/watch?v=Xt6lQAe8ues.

Moreland, J. P. "Arguing God from Consciousness?" *Closer to Truth*. https://www.closertotruth.com/interviews/2749.

Myers, Jeremy. "Crucifixion, the Spiritual Sufferings of Jesus." *Redeeming God*. https://redeeminggod.com/crucifixion-spiritual-suffering-of-jesus/.

Open Doors. "Christian Persecution." https://www.opendoorsusa.org/christian-persecution.

Oxford English Dictionary Online. "Probation." https://www.oed.com/view/Entry/2F 151705.

People & Songs. "Psalm 23 (I Am Not Alone) [Live at Linger Conference] People & Songs ft Josh Sherman." *YouTube*, April 19, 2018. https://www.youtube.com/watch?v=8OlMGnPUAdw.

Rana, Fazale. *The Cell's Design: How Chemistry Reveals the Creator's Artistry*. Grand Rapids: Baker, 2008.

Ritenbaugh, John W. "What Sin Is & What Sin Does." *Church of the Great God*, February 1996. http://www.cgg.org/index.cfm/fuseaction/Library.sr/CT/PERSONAL/k/489/What-Sin-Is-Does.htm.

Ryken, L., et al. "Redemption." In *Dictionary of Biblical Imagery*, edited by L. Ryken et al., 699. Electronic edition. Downers Grove: InterVarsity, 2000.

———. "Salvation." In *Dictionary of Biblical Imagery*, edited by L. Ryken et al., 753. Electronic edition. Downers Grove: InterVarsity, 2000.

Samples, Kenneth Richard. *A World of Difference: Putting Christian Truth-Claims to the Worldview Test*. Grand Rapids: Baker, 2007.

San Filippo, Sara, ed. "I've Wanted to Be Adopted All the Time I've Been in Foster Care . . ." *Love What Matters*. https://www.lovewhatmatters.com/adopted-all-the-time-foster-care-single-dad-adoption-forever-family/.

Sargent, Joseph, dir. *Something the Lord Made*. New York: HBO Films, 2007.

Schmidt, Alvin J. *How Christianity Changed the World*. Grand Rapids: Zondervan, 2004.

Shadyac, Tom, dir. *Bruce Almighty*. Universal City, CA: Universal, 2003.

Shawny, George. "True Story Which Mirrors God's Atonement." *Preach Arizona*. http://www.preacharizona.com/2013/01/true-story-which-mirrors-gods-atonement.html.

Smith, Christopher R. "Was It a Sin for David to Have Many Wives?" *Good Question*, February 13, 2021. https://goodquestionblog.com/2021/02/13/was-it-a-sin-for-david-to-have-many-wives.

Spielberg, Steven, dir. *Saving Private Ryan*. Universal City, CA: DreamWorks, 1998.

Stafford, Tim. *Knowing the Face of God*. Colorado Springs: NavPress, 1996.

Strange, Daniel. *Making Faith Magnetic*. Epsom, UK: The Good Book Company, 2021.

Strobel, Lee. *The Case for Heaven*. Grand Rapids: Zondervan, 2021.

Velarde, Robert. "Greatness and Wretchedness." *CRI*, June 11, 2009. https://www.equip.org/article/greatness-and-wretchedness/.

Vision Video. "The Tabernacle." *YouTube*, November 16, 2020. https://www.youtube.com/watch?v=dEqCl5n3Bis.

The Voice of the Martyrs. "Home." persecution.com.

Williams, Jimmy. "Are the Biblical Documents Reliable?" https://www.cru.org/content/dam/cru/legacy/2012/04/williamsarethebiblicaldocumentsreliable.pdf.

Winsor, Morgan, and James Bwala. "More Chibok Girls Have Escaped from Boko Haram almost 7 Years Later, Parents Say." *ABC News*, January 29, 2021. https://abcnews.go.com/International/chibok-girls-escaped-boko-haram-years-parents/story?id=75560018.

Wright, N. T. *Simply Christian*. San Francisco: HarperSanFrancisco, 2006.

Yancey, Philip. *Disappointment with God*. Grand Rapids: Zondervan, 1988.

———. *Rumors of Another World*. Grand Rapids: Zondervan, 2003.

www.ingramcontent.com/pod-product-compliance
Lightning Source LLC
Chambersburg PA
CBHW070927160426
43193CB00011B/1594